W9-AHF-709

RHYTHMS OF THE INNER LIFE

RHYTHMS OF THE INNER LIFE

YEARNING FOR CLOSENESS WITH GOD

HOWARD R. MACY

Chariot Victor Publishing
A Division of Cook Communications

Chariot Victor Publishing
Cook Communications, Colorado Springs, Colorado 80918
Cook Communications, Paris, Ontario, Canada
Kingsway Communications, Eastbourne, England

Unless otherwise noted, Scripture quotations are from *The Jerusalem Bible,* Copyright © 1966, 1967, 1968 by Darton, Longman & Todd, Ltd. and Doubleday & Company, Inc. Reprinted by permission of the publisher. Other quotations are from the *King James Version* of the Bible (KJV); the *Revised Standard Version* of the Bible (RSV), Copyright © 1946, 1952, 1971, by the Division of Christian Education of the National Council of the Churches of Christ in the United States of America. Used by permission. All rights reserved; the *Holy Bible: New International Version*® (NIV). Copyright © 1973, 1978, 1984 by the International Bible Society. Used by permission of Zondervan Bible Publishers; and the *New American Standard Bible* (NASB), © The Lockman Foundation 1960, 1962, 1963, 1968, 1971, 1972, 1973, 1975, 1977.

Cover and Interior Design: Image Studios
Cover Photography: Photodisc

© 1988, 1992, 1999 by Howard R. Macy. All rights reserved.
Printed in the United States of America.

1 2 3 4 5 6 7 8 9 10 Printing / Year 03 02 01 00 99

Library of Congress Cataloging-in-Publication Data
Macy, Howard R.
    Rythms of the inner life: yearning for closeness with God /
Howard R. Macy.
        p. cm.
    Includes bibliographical references
    ISBN 1-56476-777-9
    1. Praise of God. 2. God—Worship and love. I. Title.
BV4817.M24   1999
248.4—dc21
                                                    99-17424
                                                    CIP

No part of this book may be reproduced without permission, except for brief quotations in books and critical reviews. For more information, write Chariot Victor Publishing, 4050 Lee Vance View, Colorado Springs, Colorado 80918.

To Margi,
faith companion,
wise friend.

ACKNOWLEDGMENTS

Though writing a book is often a lonely task, it is one that thrives on the help and encouragement of others.

Many friends have given both generously, and I hope they will excuse me where I have resisted their wisdom. Colleagues at Friends University, particularly those in the Center for Christian Writers, have heartened me on many occasions. Heidi Jo Ann Carter, Richard J. Foster, D. Elton Trueblood, and Jan Wood have offered particularly insightful critiques and suggestions. My parents, Mahlon and Hazel Macy, have believed it possible, and my wife, Margi, and children, Nathan and Hannah, have endured it with grace and tenderness. For all these friends, each a gift from God, I am deeply grateful.

CONTENTS

FOREWORD

Howard Macy's book has been produced with the strong conviction that emphasis upon the merely contemporary will never suffice, either in the spiritual life or in anything else of importance. If we are only contemporary, we are inevitably shallow! Professor Macy believes that our generation needs acquaintance with the classics of devotion and that the Psalms are the greatest of all devotional classics.

Many people suppose that they know the Psalms, when as a matter of fact they do not. If as a consequence of the publication of the present volume, any considerable number of readers are led to turn directly to the Psalms, the spiritual gain may justify the work of both author and publisher.

Howard Macy is a rare combination in our generation: He combines a high level of scholarship with an unashamed piety. His scholarship does not render the piety dull, and the piety does not render the level of scholarship anything other than excellent. My own contact with Professor Macy has been primarily during his graduate student days at Earlham and Harvard. When Harvard University awarded the doctor of philosophy degree, the author's academic standing was assured. One result of the arduous work at Harvard is that Dr. Macy, in his study of the Psalms, is not limited to English translations of the ancient Hebrew poetry.

The reader will soon note that the book includes some use of the first person singular pronoun. This is employed, not for the sake of personal exposure, but in order to emphasize the empirical character of true religion. The volume, therefore, is not a *discussion* about religion, but rather a *demonstration* of it.

The hope at every point is that the serious reader may be encouraged to move from discussion *about* God to a deeper acquaintance *with Him*. Because the purpose of writing is to make a difference in human lives, the success of this book will be measured by the spiritual renewal that it helps to engender. If some readers are emancipated from a shallow modernity, the author will be amply rewarded.

The Psalms are, indeed, a priceless treasure, but a new approach to them is required if contemporary men and women are to appreciate both their depth and their relevance to our lives at the dawn of a new millennium. My own hope is that, because of this book, many readers will understand how priceless the treasure is.

D. ELTON TRUEBLOOD

INTRODUCTION

Let earth praise Yahweh:
sea-monsters and all the deeps.

Psalm 148:7

Perhaps it's surprising to think of sea monsters in the Bible. But there they are, called to sing praise to God along with the stars, the wind and hail, fruit trees and thornbushes, kings and peasants, and all the rest of creation. My picture of them is admittedly medieval and serpentine, yet I love to imagine a whole chorus of sea monsters singing, ringing barbershop chords, bouncing through great oratorio refrains, or even bellowing a bit of rock or gospel. I see them strain, necks abulge, to raise enthusiastic choruses of praise, for such eager extravagance is only fitting in honor of the gracious Creator. And I want to join them.

I want to join other singers in the Bible, too. The singers who thirst for God, those who are nearly speechless in wonder, those bowed by despair, those who speak unflinchingly of trust—all of them sing songs like those my heart—and yours—has known. They sing of the deep currents of the life with God that has been known by all who have dwelt in the Eternal, whether patriarchs or prophets, apostles or modern believers. They sing of the movements of the heart.

In this book I want to explore seven movements of the heart: longing, waiting, trembling, despairing, resting, conversing, and celebrating. These are inward movements, rather than outward disciplines. They are responses to our experience of God, rather than practices of religious devotion. It would be misleading, however, to separate entirely the spiritual disciplines and the movements of the heart, for the disciplines, properly understood, are means that can lead us ever more deeply into these inner realities. Indeed, in each chapter I shall suggest specific practices that can nurture our responses to God.

The rhythms of the inner life as I discuss them here do not comprise a seven-step program to bliss. I have chosen a sequence to suggest how one progresses in the inner life, but it should not be taken too rigidly. At times these movements go forward in a concurrent and complementary way. During some periods, one may take prominence over the others, but all are part of the cycle of our experience with God.

Bishops and beggars, princes and peasants have, over the centuries, witnessed to this life, and we shall use their testimony to teach us. Out of this great company of the faithful, however, we shall pay particular attention to the ancient Hebrew singers who gave us the Psalms of the Old Testament. Composed over a period of several hundred years, these magnificent songs have endured now well over two millennia as a primary guide to the inner life, and for all their marks of antiquity, they are still fresh and striking today.

"The enduring appeal of the Psalms," writes Elton Trueblood, "means that the common man in various generations feels that these songs say what he would like to say also, if only he could."[1] For this reason, these songs have not only filled temple and synagogue, but have also echoed through the halls of monasteries during the night offices and resounded in the sanctuaries of Calvin's Geneva. They have for centuries been at the heart of *The Book of Common Prayer* and of hymnody. Though the great tune "Old Hundredth" still survives, the Psalms' ancient lyrics are continually set to a new culture's tunes, with "Bless the Lord!" now appearing in folk and rock songs and even on Broadway.

It matters very little that these ancient singers had camels instead of cars, open fires instead of microwave ovens, and simple lyres instead of pipe organs. They knew God deeply, and in the timelessness of what they knew is a rich resource for our own faith The psalmists live on in their songs, to be our teachers.

Our interest in nurturing the inner life gives shape to this work. In using the Psalms, the book is thematic and selective. It is not a commentary. Nor is it a rational defense of the authenticity of the life of faith. These chapters are for those who have entered this life and those who wish to live in its adventure. I hope to help them describe and understand what they are discovering and to point toward regions they may not yet have explored. For those who have not yet joined this life, I hope this book will be an invitation, not as a slick-paper, hard-sell promotion, but through the simple witness of ordinary citizens of God's Kingdom, through the timeless testimony of people who have known God.

Alleluia!

Let heaven praise Yahweh:
praise him, heavenly heights,
praise him, all his angels,
praise him, all his armies!

Praise him, sun and moon,
praise him, shining stars,
praise him, highest heavens,
and waters above the heavens!

Let them all praise the name of Yahweh,
at whose command they were created;
he has fixed them in their place forever,
by an unalterable statute.

Let earth praise Yahweh.
sea-monsters and all the deeps,
fire and hail, snow and mist,
gales that obey his decree,

mountains and hills,
orchards and forests,
wild animals and farm animals,
snakes and birds,

all kings on earth and nations,
princes, all rulers in the world,
young men and girls,
old people, and children too!

Let them all praise the name of Yahweh,
for his name and no other is sublime,
transcending earth and heaven in majesty,
raising the fortunes of his people,
to the praises of the devout,
of Israel, the people dear to him.

Psalm 148

ONE

LONGING

As a doe longs
for running streams,
so longs my soul
for you, my God.

Psalm 42:1

During a July week in Kansas, when daily the temperatures soared to 110 degrees, the sky hardened into a vast sun shield, and the winds withered the grass, eight of my relatives showed up from softer climes. Shortly after they arrived, the well, our only source of water, went dry. Though a long hose and the generosity of our neighbors met our urgent need, we quickly began to drill anew to the streams flowing thirty feet below our lawn. This ill-timed predicament, once safely past, reminded me of a similar crisis in my own spiritual state.

In that year and, it seemed, just as abruptly, my inner well went dry, too. After finishing several weeks filled with teaching, preaching, retreat leadership, and other public ministries, apparently well received, I looked inward to find only wilderness. My own spirit was arid, and even trying to bring words of life to others stirred up scorching winds rather than moist breezes. Every effort smacked of mere training and idle wordcraft, "leaky cisterns" at best; and I knew that my well was clogged, corroded by carelessness, blocking the flow of the waters of God's life. Steady longing for God had given way to complacency. A schedule filled with worthwhile activities had elbowed aside yearning. Now, parched and barren, I thirsted and longed to know anew God's Presence springing up like En-gedi in Judah's wilderness, cascading down into refreshing pools, giving life to all that stays near.

My craving for God felt like that of the psalmists. *Thirsting. Seeking. Yearning.* Words of intensity and appetite run through ancient Israel's songs, and rightly so, for an insatiable longing for God must be the first and constant movement of any heart that wants to know God. Without seeking, there is no finding. So with the psalmists I pleaded, "Like thirsty ground I yearn for you" (143:6), and I learned again the truth of their promise, "How happy those who . . . seek him with their whole heart" (119:2).

This image of the seeking heart appears frequently in the Psalms, but because we often fail to capture its sense, we also fail to see its power. On the one hand, wholehearted seeking is much more than a preface to the life of faith. Over the years I have known self-declared "finders" who regard seeking as part of their past, an act that, once having brought them to faith, is now behind them. On the other hand, I have also known "seekers" who hold a tenacious skepticism about ever finding. But I am not talking here of finders who won't seek and seekers who won't find. Instead I join the psalmists in pointing to the seeking of those who have already found, who know God directly and not by hearsay. "I have tasted you," confessed Augustine, "and I hunger and thirst after you."[1] Precisely such seeking born of discovery is the taproot of life as a friend of God.

When we come to know God, we throw open the door to a vast new universe in our consciousness, a cosmos of divine love, presence, and joy. This universe reaches beyond our wildest imagination and, even as it overwhelms us, plants in us the conviction that we haven't yet begun to explore the galaxies of its mysteries. Often as I have pursued this life I have seen myself coming to a door in the world of wonder that I have known. As I throw it open, I am astonished to be standing on the threshold of a world vaster and more wondrous still, feeling my little world of experience dwarfed, just as is the earth when seen among stars, black holes, and galaxies. Yet the discovery doesn't end there. I am drawn to still other doors, opening onto even grander worlds, until I see that the universe of God's life is inexhaustibly rich and that I have scarcely begun to know it. My experience is like that of perennial students who jest that the more they learn, the less they know. But rather than coming as a taunt or rebuke, this taste of knowing God stands as an invitation to enter and explore what now escapes even our imaginations.

A wonder-filled seeking springs up, then, which makes us eager to know all of God that we can. It prevents us from being satisfied with just a taste of the goodness of God. It calls us beyond desiring only the assurance that we are "saved," content merely to be acquitted before the Divine Judge, instead of longing to know the Friend who is dearer than life itself. Our hunger and thirst have been satisfied, as Jesus promised, but the sheer joy of it all causes us to hunger and thirst all the more. Here, then, is the seeking that is yearning for God—even obsession with God—because becoming God's friend is more compelling than any other desire or duty.

Religion without passion is a deadly fraud. Without urgency or desire, faith neither lives nor gives life. Yet a great deal of modern religion, regardless of theological stripe, ignores this central truth. Too often contemporary worship and devotion are merely polite and proper, closely guarded and genteel. Tame, well-mannered religion, however, has no root in life, either in the Divine Life or in our own. That is why the command to love God with every shred of our being is the first and greatest commandment. It stands not only at the core of faithfulness, but also at the center of life itself. The heart must throb for God.

"Religion without passion is a deadly fraud. Without urgency or desire, faith neither lives nor gives life."

Such a desire for God contrasts sharply with many religious passions that abound today. Some have ravenous appetites for watchdogging true doctrine. Others are eager to build their congregations, while still others serve God to ensure their own happiness and success. But in all of this, where is the deep yearning to know God? "This people approaches me only in words, honours me only with lip-service while its heart is far from me," God once charged Israel (Isaiah 29:13), and the indictment still sticks. This, too, is a day of jangling praise but distant hearts. All those who would cry, "Lord, Lord!" must also long to know God.

Some will object, I am sure, that such yearning is simply a matter of style and temperament, a religious emotionalism suitable for some but not necessary for all. Such objections, however, miss the mark. Longing for God does not require adopting certain rituals, formal or informal, or working up certain emotional states. It is not a holy swoon, any more than loving God is pious puppy love. Longing for God is a steady movement of the heart, one that runs deeper than any action or emotion. This longing is the root of any significant spiritual growth, and it must not be dismissed flippantly as mere style or temperament. We differ widely, of course, in our practices of devotion and in religious feeling, and each of us experiences cycles in religious emotion and intensity. Yet the eagerness to know God, the sense of need to be drawn further into the Divine Life, animates any vital relationship with God.

The psalmist's words show us well this life of longing:

> *God, you are my God, I am seeking you,*
> *my soul is thirsting for you,*
> *my flesh is longing for you, a land parched,*
> *weary and waterless; I long to gaze on you in the*
> *Sanctuary, and to see your power and glory.*

> —*Psalm 63:1-2*

Here three lively metaphors commonly used in the Psalms describe the character of the life of longing: thirst for God, eagerness to be in God's presence in the temple, and anticipation of seeing God's face. These images can guide our own experience as they point toward urgency, toward our experience of the presence of God, and toward the sense of risk that the life of longing inevitably entails.

The Answering Thirst

A maddeningly effective television advertisement for a soft drink once showed an old-time cowboy bursting through the doors of a saloon, after a long day on the trail. Dust was his buddy at the bar, following him into the room and exploding into the air when the wrangler banged open his saddlebags to pull out a bag of potato chips. When that hot, parched cowboy started eating the potato chips, I and millions of other viewers braced ourselves to rush to get something cold to drink. Exactly on cue, just as I reached the kitchen door, a cold bottle of the soft drink appeared on the screen. I usually didn't have what they advertised, but they had succeeded in making me feel as if I must have a drink right now. It worked every time.

Because we all know thirst, we can grasp how, for the psalmists, the language of thirst evoked both urgency and necessity. They are eager, even desperate, for God: "As a doe longs for running streams, so longs my soul for you, my God. My soul thirsts for God, the God of life" (42:1-2). It is a thirst like that of the cracked earth pleading through its brittle, mosaic surface for rain: "My soul is thirsting for you . . . a land parched, weary and waterless" (63:1); "I stretch out my hands, like thirsty ground I yearn for you" (143:6). The same urgent sense of need must characterize those who would progress in the inner life. Knowing God is not merely pleasant, but pressing. It is not a luxury, but a matter of life and death. How, asks the seeker, can I even exist without the life-giving waters that flow from God?

I will always remember the cold waters of a spring that a fishing buddy introduced me to several years ago. As he drove over the lower reaches of Oregon's Mount Hood, he would always stop to drink at this spring, fill his gallon jug, and grin broadly as he bragged about its refreshing taste. He would grin again as we later quenched our thirst from the jug, tired from casting to trout on the mighty Deschutes River. No weather, no flurry of fishing, no emergency, could deter him from stopping at that little spring. His delight and eagerness were simply too great. It is this kind of eager thirst that also opens the door to the inner life. This is a thirst driven by satisfaction, rather than disappointment. What we have tasted is so remarkable that we must have more, and we know somehow that we can never have enough. "All we taste, against all we lack, is like a single drop of water against the whole sea," wrote John Ruysbroeck, "for we feed upon His Immensity, which we cannot devour, and we yearn after His Infinity, which we cannot attain."[2]

Precisely because the urgency and intensity of thirst are essential to any life truly open to God, Scripture and tradition are filled with images and examples of what this means. It is to love God with our whole being. It is to lose our lives in order to save them. It is the psalmist singing, "I look to no one else in heaven, I delight in nothing else on earth. My flesh and my heart are pining with love, my heart's Rock, my own, God for ever!" (73:25-26). It is Paul's straining forward to reach the goal, laying aside every weight. It is Francis of Assisi, praying through the whole night the simple but profound words, "My God and my all. My God and my all."[3] It is Kierkegaard's purity of heart that wills one thing.[4] It is the exhilarating recklessness of abandoning ourselves to God.

The seeking for God that is born of discovery has a hound-like quality. Once we've caught the scent and, perhaps, broken the leash, we'll eagerly follow the trail, wherever it might lead, nose down, through field and bramble, water and shrub, in the hope of cornering our quarry. To have come to know God at all is to have been given the scent, and though we know well that we will hardly tree the Holy One, we also know that this is the trail we must follow. So we rush on as fast as our noses will take us, and we would do well to bay with excitement as we go.

Those who recall Francis Thompson's haunting image of God as the Hound of Heaven, pursuing us down the halls of time, might well ask who, in fact, is the hound and who the quarry, whether we seek God or whether we are sought. If we try to answer the question on those terms, however, we stray into theological foolishness. What we discover, instead, is that all the while we have been pursuing God, he has been rushing toward us with reckless love, arms flung wide to hug us home. God aches for every person, for every creature, indeed, for every scrap of life in all creation to be joined again in the unity that was its first destiny. So while we are crying out, "Where are you, God?" the divine voice echoes through our hiding places, "Where are *you*?" Indeed, the story of the Garden of Eden reminds us that it is God who calls out first, and to this we answer. God's yearning for us stirs up our longing in response. God's initiating presence may be ever so subtle—an inward tug of desire, a more-than-coincidence meeting of words and events, a glimpse of the beyond in a storm or in a flower—but it is enough to make the heart skip a beat and to make us want to know more.

The life of longing, then, is a response to God's wooing. And it is necessary if we expect to come to know God. We do not slight grace to insist that we must take responsibility for our life with God. Indeed, it is precisely the failure to long persistently for God that stunts spiritual growth and produces what Juan Carlos Ortiz calls "the permanent childhood of the believer."[5] A profound, life-giving knowledge of God is not the privilege of only a chosen few, but of all who perpetually seek it. The mystics, writes Evelyn Underhill, knew God as "a living Presence and Love . . . not because he loved and attended to them more than he does to us; but because they loved and attended to him more than we do."[6]

"The life of longing is not a week's or a month's journey. It is not a short course culminating in instant bliss or saint-hood. It must be our whole lives."

Just as we both seek and are sought, so we must nurture the life of longing as well as receive it as a gift. Sometimes this life will flow easily; at other times it grows strong only through steady discipline. At no time should we judge its value or health by our momentary emotional state. I can hardly overemphasize this in a time when many people hook their faith to easy, cliché-ridden answers, to the desire for instant results, and sometimes, to emotional roller coasters. Too often people who begin seeking God are disappointed when they don't see results come right away or in precisely the way they expect or have been told to expect. Many then give up the search, thinking it boring or fruitless or, perhaps, thinking themselves failures or unlikely candidates for such a way of living. The life of longing, however, is not a week's or a month's journey. It is not a short course culminating in instant bliss or sainthood. It must be our whole lives, a way of persistence, of experimentation, of growth, of insight, and of even further enchantment and puzzlement by the Mystery that is God. Those who know God deeply teach this point best, for it seems that those who have learned the most are the very ones who insist on how much they yet need to learn and who most long for God. To expect to achieve in an instant what the saints have pursued for a lifetime easily misleads and disappoints us.

Eagerness and Fanaticism

Though I am eager to encourage a spirit of devotion and not to dictate legalistic exercises of devotion, I can propose several approaches to nurture the life of longing, some of which are suggested by the psalmists themselves.

One way of seeking that the psalmists show us is to be eager to understand and follow God's teaching and guidance. "I long for you, Yahweh, my saviour, your Law is my delight" (119:174), a verse characteristic of this great Torah Psalm, clearly couples longing for God with longing for instruction. Though modern readers struggle to understand the Law as anything but a straitjacket legalism or harsh taskmaster, even a little reading of the Psalms themselves shows that these singers delighted in the Law as a gracious guide and welcome light on the path of life. The word we translate *Law* comes from a Hebrew word for "teaching and learning," and it is in that spirit that we can best appreciate it and learn to share the psalmists' longing for God's guidance. In our own search, we, like them, can come to know divine instruction through the Bible and through a direct, conversational relationship with God.

Though the Bible itself does not claim to be our only source to point us to God, it is an indispensable guide, particularly if we can move beyond seeing it as a magical religious encyclopedia. We must come to know it instead as a book about life and faith in a rough-and-tumble world like our own. In it we see the traces of the Presence among us, the trail of God's loving pursuit. Here we observe the strata where the river of God's life has flowed, cutting through, shaping, and transforming. Here, too, we read words, still probing and inviting, from men and women carried along in that life. So as we read the Bible regularly, with fresh and varied approaches, it can guide us in important ways.

One way, and this is the guidance that we commonly expect, is through direct teaching. We, like the psalmists, can love and meditate on the Torah day and night, because it shows us the character and purposes of God as well as our own potential and responsibilities. Yet the life of longing may be aided equally by the stories of the Bible's people. The Bible is filled with the stories of the seekers and the sought, who encourage us through both their faithfulness and their failures. There is Moses hotfooting it to see the burning bush and shuffling and mumbling to stay out of Egypt. There is that classic model of faithfulness, Abraham, who risked leaving family and country, with not so much as a travel guide, lying through his teeth to save his own skin and figuring all the angles he could to help God fulfill the divine promise. While sinking up to his armpits in a dark cistern's slime, surely Jeremiah wished he had won on day one, when he sputtered objections while the Almighty crammed his mouth full of words. For him, knowing God was like an unquenchable fire in his bones. Yet despite the days when he wished his father's "It's a boy" cigars had exploded, he never could escape the living truth of God's first promise, "Don't be afraid, I'll be with you," as he felt faithful love pursuing and empowering him. Such "heroes of faith," as we now call them, are a lot like us, both seeking and sought, and there is a gallery full of them to teach us about the life of longing. Paul wrote that their examples were "meant to teach us something about hope" since we see in them "how people who did not give up were helped by God" (Romans 15:4).

Because God wants to teach us, too, we can, if we will, learn to know God ourselves. Becoming God's friend, however, requires more of us than simply knowing about God and about faithful men and women who have gone before us. It will take time and eagerness, just as any relationship does. No wonder I feel blocked when I discover that I am more eager to analyze Moses' and Jeremiah's objections to obedience than to overcome my own. No wonder my spirit seems dry when I neglect conversing with God in prayer. For it is only in giving ourselves energetically to developing an intimate relationship with God, one in which we can hear the divine voice in fresh and lively ways, that we can even begin to understand the experience of the "heroes of faith." Only through steady devotion can we come to know God ourselves.

Of course, what seems a million distractions to divert us from the life of longing come to all of us. Bills, laundry, and dishes stack up. Kids need to be carted, and shopping needs to be done. There are committees and dinners, parties and choirs. And the boss wants "can-do" zealots to pile extra effort on extra effort. In the midst of it all, "next week," when it will be better, seems as near and as remote as the next millennium. We are all susceptible, whether our distractions are outer busyness or inner scatteredness, ambition, or other temptations. What I experience as a teacher I see even in some pastors, who get so involved in doing religious work, creating successful churches, and pleasing people that they, too, know God only as a casual acquaintance, instead of as an intimate Friend. The pressures against the life of longing are very great, but we are not, by and large, merely victims. Our overriding choice can still be to know God.

A poster on my office wall often brings me up short in the midst of my daily rush and inner clatter and sets me back on the necessary way. It says simply, "Give God time." That time might be given over to any number of things—quiet, prayer, meditation, a gentle thanksgiving walk, study, holy emptiness—but there must be time. Longing for God must be so important that we create that time, partly by giving it priority over what others expect of us and over our own ambitions and social calendars. We must not procrastinate and let longing for God fall on the slag heap of "important but not urgent" tasks that so many of us fail to complete. We must not allow lesser things to steal away time with God.

"A poster on my office wall often brings me up short in the midst of my daily rush and inner clatter and sets me back on the necessary way. It says simply, 'Give God time.'"

Some shy away from this life because they fear fanaticism. Frankly, fanaticism seems to have a bright future, for there is always enough bona fide craziness in the name of religion both to amuse scoffers and to embarrass the faithful. Nobody wants any part of it, and it helps only a little to know that some of today's fanatics may well be tomorrow's saints. We suspect that they may just as easily become long-term patients in a mental hospital. Even if we dare to acknowledge that today Jeremiah, Ezekiel, and even Jesus (Mark 3:21; John 10:20) would probably qualify for psychiatric examinations, our question remains, "Do I have to be a fanatic to seek God with my entire self? Will I wind up being a religious drunk with a sacramental lampshade on my head?"

When I feel such questions sending caution signals in my heart, I soon have to admit that they rise up mostly out of my pride. I have not fully learned how, like Saint Francis, to rejoice in my own humiliation. I would much rather be liked than laughed at. So I would prefer to hear the answer, "No, you don't have to be a fanatic. God doesn't like lampshades on the heads of the faithful, even if they have the divine name written all over them." But though God intends neither to make sport of us nor to guide us into religious foolishness that is merely unholy nonsense, to say no holds us back rather than urges us on. It allows us to rest complacently, with a sigh of relief, instead of panting with eagerness for the life of God.

To the question, "Do I have to be a fanatic?" we might also answer, "I don't know." That's obvious. None of us knows precisely what faithfulness will require, and frankly, God's wisdom often appears foolish in the eyes of myopic cultures. Yet that is little comfort to us when we look eager devotion in the eye and see there unpredictability or even a glint of wildness.

Ultimately we must say, "Yes, you have to be a fanatic." Any devotion to God worthy of the name must be obsessive in a profound sense. It must be the controlling factor, the fixed reference point, in all of one's life. It must even risk excess. To love God above all else has always seemed unreasonable, irrational, even fanatical, to many, but it is precisely in the reckless abandonment of ourselves to God, in giving up our control, and in risking our respectability that we emerge into life. Nothing less will do. This, then, is the fanaticism that is necessary—not pious idiocy, but consuming passion for God.

The Penetrating Presence

When they sang of their eagerness to be in the temple, the psalmists spoke in another way of their longing for God. "How I rejoiced when they said to me, 'Let us go to the house of Yahweh!'" (122:1), they sang, and added "a single day in your courts is worth more than a thousand elsewhere" (84:10).

Such expressions of joy at being in the temple abound in the Psalms, and they should be seen as evidence of the singers' delight in being with God. Unfortunately, modern readers have often trivialized these deep longings by using them to crowbar people out of their easy chairs and shoehorn them into the pews. The Psalms have no interest, however, in promoting church attendance or enhancing statistical reports. Instead, they express the singers' passion to be in the presence of God.

The Hebrews, of course, did not believe that their God was confined to the precincts of the temple. After all, that would hardly be fitting for the Maker of Heaven and Earth, the One who calls each star by name and barks out the commands for their marching drills. Without limiting the divine majesty, however, Israelite worshipers did believe that God was present in a special way in the temple. This was the place God had chosen to put his Name, a symbol of divine presence and power. This is where the Glory of God, with all its fiery, smoke-shrouded brilliance, dwelt. God had chosen this holy place as the center from which Torah would be declared to the peoples of the world. To long to be in the temple, then, was to long for the presence of God.

The depth of that longing for the Presence is seen most vividly, perhaps, in Psalm 84. The singer's desire bursts out, "How I love your palace, Yahweh Sabaoth! How my soul yearns and pines for Yahweh's courts!" (84:1-2). Indeed, his eagerness is so great that he clearly envies, if not resents, the sparrows who, by nesting in the nooks and crannies of the temple's rafters, get to stay in the Presence all the time. In the ritual practice of some of Israel's neighbors, worshipers would leave human figurines, wide-eyed alabaster statues, in their temples, to be present for them while they went about the daily tasks of sowing seed and shearing sheep. But that would not satisfy the devout Hebrew whose one request was "to live in the house of Yahweh all the days of my life, to enjoy the sweetness of Yahweh and to consult him in his temple" (27:4).

Though we may not wholly share the psalmists' idea of where God may be encountered, we can still join in their desire to stand continually in the presence of God, for this is another gateway to the life of devotion. One way we can develop this dimension of the life of longing is to increase our awareness that God is really among us. Taking a broad view, we can heighten our often diminished sense that it is indeed in God whom we "live and move and have our being" (Acts 17:28, RSV). But we can also focus more narrowly to see how God comes to us in our own experience. "Listen to your life," Frederick Buechner urges, and it is good counsel.[7] If we would but reflect on it, for example, most of us could recall instances of God's protection and preparation, perhaps unrecognized at the time, which later proved providential. The psalmists did just that as they linked their awareness of God at work with their yearning: "I recall the days of old, I reflect on all that you did, I ponder your deeds; I stretch out my hands, like thirsty ground I yearn for you" (143:5-6). If we take seriously the biblical view that God comes to us in the midst of our ordinary living, then we can learn to observe the workings of the holy in our commonness. Part of the genius of the giants of faith is how clearly they saw God's Presence penetrating everyday life.

Two ways of improving our vision of God at work are listening prayer, which I will discuss in the next chapter, and keeping a spiritual journal. Faithfully keeping even a simple journal can produce a bumper crop of growth and insight. In this private journal one goes well beyond "Dear Diary" entries by recording events, feelings, questions, insights, prayer projects, puzzlements, testing of divine leadings, prayers, and whatever else seems suitable. I find that the act of writing itself helps to bring my experience into focus and to distill what God has been teaching me. Beyond its immediate benefit, over time my journal also reveals how God has responded to my prayers, whether I have indeed abandoned my anger at those who have hurt me, what things God has had to teach a slow learner like me over and over again, and much more. There are several fine introductions to this practice, but with or without instruction, honest seeking through journaling can make us more aware of God's nearness and more eager to join in God's purposes for us. Careful listening to our lives helps us know God.

Not only can we learn to see God's Presence, we can invite it. We can "practice the Presence of God." Perhaps this phrase is best known from Brother Lawrence, who discovered that he could know God's Presence as fully while working in the kitchen as when observing the regular offices of prayer. Frank Laubach tried to recover this same reality in his "Game with Minutes" in which he tried to see in how many minutes of each hour he could consciously think of God. Even with uneven success, Laubach discovered that he was "communing with the very God of the universe itself" and that his experience was so rich that he "ached with bliss" and knew what it was to open his soul to "entertain the glory of God."[8] Similarly, the simple Russian, Pilgrim, constantly prayed the Jesus Prayer, "Lord Jesus Christ, have mercy on me," until it became as natural to him as breathing.[9] Many others have been helped by praying often Agnes Sanford's adaptation of that prayer, "Lord Jesus Christ, fill me with your light and love."[10] I have found it helpful to talk with God conversationally as I drive, while walking to school, in my office, and in many other little ways in the midst of my daily activities. These are simple means, but potentially very powerful. Through them the Glory and the Presence, which the ancient singers longed constantly to know, can penetrate every minute and flood our hearts.

The Transforming Risk

A bold picture of longing, closely related to their desire for God's Presence, is the psalmists' eagerness to see the face of God. Of course the Hebrews, who permitted no images of their God, understood the outrageousness of this way of speaking, but they still used it to convey their longing for God. The singers urge their hearers to "seek his face untiringly" (105:4) and pray, "Lord, I do seek your face, do not hide your face from me" (see 27:8-9). In many cases, the desire to see the face of God probably means simply to be in the temple. At other times, however, the singers understand it as a symbol of both intimacy and of awesome danger.

On the one hand, the Hebrews pleaded with God not to hide his face or turn a cold shoulder to them, for they knew what it meant to have the Lord gaze on them in tenderness, in singular attention, in unquestioning acceptance. They blessed one another with words from Moses, "The Lord make his face shine upon you and be gracious to you; the Lord turn his face toward you and give you peace" (Numbers 6:25-26, NIV). Convinced of the majesty of God's love, it is little wonder that they would yearn to stand under the warm, steady gaze of the Almighty, to see God's face and to be seen.

On the other hand, says an important Old Testament tradition, to see the face of God is an awesome and dangerous experience. It could kill you. Small wonder, then, that Isaiah thought he was a dead man when in his vision he saw Yahweh enthroned in the sanctuary (Isaiah 6) and that Moses was told that, even when crouched behind a mountain rock and shielded by God's hand, he could dare see only God's back passing by (Exodus 33). The fact that Jacob, Isaiah, Moses, and others did see God's face and survive in no way diminishes the wonder of the encounter. After God spoke with Moses "face to face, as a man speaks with his friend," the lingering radiance on Moses' face was so bright that the Israelites wouldn't come near him (Exodus 33:11; 34:29-35).

Similar experiences of meeting God face-to-face are recorded in later tradition, although most of us scarcely comprehend them. For example, it is reported of Brother Giles, one of Saint Francis' companions, that for over two weeks he had visions of the Lord so overwhelming that he thought he was dying. The dazzling brightness and the bliss were so stunning that he cried aloud and prayed "fervently to the Lord not to place such a burden on him."[11]

We should not discount such language and reports too quickly, just because of the poverty of our own experience. After all, contemporary culture predisposes us to dismiss even the possibility of such experiences, and I suspect most of us have not sought God seriously enough to expect such powerful encounters. Though some experiences with the Holy One may come unbidden, it is unlikely that we will see the face of God if we do not earnestly seek it.

To see danger in the metaphor of "seeing God's face" reveals both the psalmists' eagerness and our caution. Simply put, there is risk in wanting to see God's face. This sense of risk, it seems to me, shows even more clearly the intensity of the psalmists' longing for God. In their single-mindedness, knowing God was worth any risk. Nothing else mattered.

More halfhearted than single-minded, it is precisely the anticipation of risk that holds many of us back. We don't like risk, and even though the frontiers of spiritual growth require it, we prefer to avoid it. Not only would we like to have the frontiers of the spirit scouted out for us, we would also like to have the frontier fully tamed and settled, like a new suburban development with well-lighted streets and sewers installed, established zoning codes, houses built and finished save for seeding the lawn and planting the shrubs, shopping centers nearby, and adequate police protection. No pioneering for us—no danger from the dark wild, no felling trees or clearing boulders so that we can plant a subsistence garden, no climbing mountain passes or fording swollen streams. We prefer comfortable safety to risk.

"The spiritual world cannot be made suburban. It is always the frontier, and if we would live in it, we must accept and even rejoice that it remains untamed."

The spiritual world, however, cannot be made suburban. It is always the frontier, and if we would live in it, we must accept and even rejoice that it remains untamed. The Ultimate Reality will not yield to our small-minded blueprints for the City of God.

Any realistic longing for God must wrestle with the apprehension that we don't know exactly what we're getting into. At times this life can be very uncomfortable, because we know that we will be changed without always knowing in what way. However, where there is discomfort, there is also security. As we pursue this life, a confidence grows that knowing God, whatever the risks, is safer and sweeter than any other path. We come to know deeply that ultimately this is not only the best but the only reasonable course.

Though we will not always live with our hearts in our throats, we should take up risk as a spiritual discipline. We need daily to yield our whole lives up to God, and we must examine them steadily to see whether we have declared any area off-limits to God's direction and transforming power. We must choose not just once but constantly to love God with all our hearts, souls, and strength, and to allow God completely to direct our living. We must choose perpetually to hold ourselves in this sometimes uncomfortable but secure place of risk.

The life of longing requires such vigilance, yet it is only by making the Lord our only joy that we can enter the life to which God still graciously calls us. "Our Lord finds our desires not too strong, but too weak," writes C.S. Lewis. "We are half-hearted creatures, fooling about with drink and sex and ambition when infinite joy is offered us. . . . We are far too easily pleased."[12] Perpetual longing is the way of promise. "How happy those who . . . seek him with their whole heart" (119:2).

T W O
WAITING

Be still before the Lord,
and wait patiently for him.

Psalm 37:7, RSV

Sometimes I get nearly worn out watching other people become spiritual. They're sincere enough, I'm sure. In fact, the ones that wear me out are usually people who have a new urgency to know God. But in their eagerness, some of them fall into a round of activity that would sap the strength of a marathoner. They go to every Bible study and prayer meeting they can find. They take up church work with a vengeance— teaching Sunday school, working on committees, evangelizing, hunting heretics—whatever the church is doing. And they adopt a stiff regimen of personal disciplines as well. The problem, of course, is not that I get tired watching, but that they get worn out, too, and often retreat from longing for God into ordinary religion or into nothing at all. They learn too late that seeking must be tempered with waiting, that eagerness must stand in tension with patience.

The devotional masters warn against a double danger in the life with God. The first is complacency, a spiritual sloth for which the life of longing is a cure. The second is "striving," a way of life so filled with religious activity and pious self-will that it drowns out the voice and thwarts the action of God. It is this second danger that the discipline of waiting effectively fights.

Waiting is not simply another religious activity to be added to the rest. Though we have methods to help us—meditation and silence, for example—waiting is more than physical silence. It is a movement of the heart, a stance we take before God. Waiting is an inner acquiescence, releasing our striving and abandoning our lives entirely to the work of God. Quieting our whole selves, we surrender our activity, our plans, and our dreams. When we wait, we yield up our expectations of what God should do, our precious hoards of ritual and doctrine, our social awareness, and our self-concepts. Waiting is totally submitting to God and inviting God to move in our hearts with complete freedom.

"Waiting is not leaning back in a rocking chair on the front porch of our hearts, watching with bemused curiosity to see if anything interesting will happen."

Even though waiting is not an outward activity, it is something that we do. It is not leaning back in a rocking chair on the front porch of our hearts, watching with bemused curiosity to see if anything interesting will happen. It is not something we inadvertently fall into, should we ever run out of activities. Instead, we choose to wait. We consciously carve out an inner space of yielded tranquillity. We hush the insistent noises of our hearts.

All of us who have fidgeted through our early experiences with silence or stillness can witness that waiting does not come easily. It requires practice and persistence. As Bernard of Clairvaux put it, "Waiting upon God is not idleness, but work which beats all other work to one unskilled in it."[1] It is a movement of the heart that can be nurtured, however, even to the point where waiting can become a gentle expectancy penetrating the hurly-burly of our days. Indeed, if waiting does not permeate even our busyness, we have not yet learned its ways.

The failure to see waiting as more than mere idleness often obscures its importance. It would be nice to have the luxury of doing nothing, many people think, but they insist that they must press on to more practical aspects of religious life. Blinded by a frantic, misguided pragmatism, they impatiently reject the work of waiting in the life of devotion, even though it is one of the most practical openings to the life with God. It is in waiting that we learn to listen to God. In waiting we become wise enough to reject "staying busy" as a goal in life and learn how better to spend our energies. We learn to see ourselves, our duty, the world, and God more truly, and that is eminently practical.

Expecting the Encounter

"Waiting patiently in expectation," says Simone Weil, "is the foundation of the spiritual life."[2] Patience and expectancy are, indeed, essential to waiting, but they easily elude us. I suppose we never entirely outgrow the spirit of a child's incessant questions while traveling: "Are we there yet? How much longer will it be?" Scarcely more sophisticated is the impatience of those who insist on setting dates for God's final triumph in history. In this and many other ways we are inclined to yield to impatience and to distort true anticipation. Waiting for God must not be a spiritual version of nervous foot shuffling, clock-watching, nail biting, or shoving at the back of the line. It does not lack eagerness, but it is patient.

The impatience that undermines waiting for God springs up in many forms. Some people are impatient with the present. Preoccupied with dreams for the future or with fears of what it might bring, they ignore or are blinded to the grace of the present moment. Others are impatient with themselves when they fail to achieve the instant spiritual maturity they had sought. While it is right to guard against stagnant self-satisfaction, it is just as important to protect ourselves from a perfectionism that constantly damns us for not yet having reached our goals. Spiritual fruit, like apples and pears, takes time to develop from blossom to full maturity.

Still others are impatient with God. One of the psalmists complains, "Worn out with calling, my throat is hoarse, my eyes are strained, looking [waiting] for my God" (69:3). Another backhandedly reveals his impatience even as he gives thanks: "I waited and waited for Yahweh, now at last he has stooped to me and heard my cry for help" (40:1). We share this timeless human condition when we demand signs from the Lord or insist on instant deliverance from all of our problems. Waiting for God means living in the confidence that God's wisdom and power outstrip our own scenarios for divine action.

One antidote for impatience is to live in hope. One psalmist clearly connects waiting and hope as he sings, "Rest in God alone my soul! He is the source of my hope" (62:5). The Hebrew noun for "hope" in this instance is related to one of the main verbs used to speak of waiting for God. In fact, several of the words used for "waiting" for God can be translated accurately as "hoping" in God. This clearly suggests that confident hope is part of waiting.

Another song pictures the sturdy expectancy of this waiting:

> *I wait for Yahweh, my soul waits for him,*
> *I rely [wait] on his promise,*
> *my soul relies [waits] on the Lord*
> *more than a watchman on the coming of dawn.*

—*Psalm 130:5-6*

These lines portray neither wavering hope that wonders whether the desired dawn will ever come nor pushiness that would seek to drag the sun over the horizon before its time. There is, instead, waiting filled with confidence and patience. In this kind of expectancy we anticipate that God will hear us, will come to us, and will transform us. Even though we may at times stand on tiptoe, straining to see God's coming, we may also sit back restfully, knowing that he will come on time.

Stilling the Noise

Besides patient expectancy, waiting for God is also to learn stillness. "Be still, and know that I am God" (46:10, RSV), invites the Holy One. *The Jerusalem Bible* translates here, "Pause a while," perhaps capturing more precisely the sense of the Hebrew verb. Drop what you are doing. Take a deep breath. Relax. "Be still, and know that I am God, exalted among the nations, exalted over the earth."

Gentleness and restfulness flood this stillness, bringing the peace one singer describes in these words:

Enough for me to keep my soul tranquil and quiet
like a child in its mother's arms,
as content as a child that has been weaned.
Israel, rely [wait] on Yahweh,
now and for always.

—Psalm 131:2-3

Imagine that waiting for God is like being a babe in arms, content to rest without squirm or scream in his mother's loving nearness! Often it is in gentle stillness, not in thunderous theophanies, that we can come to know God, overwhelming in both majesty and tenderness. Madame Guyon writes: "The interior life, that is, the inward life of the spirit, is not a place that is taken by storm or violence. That inward kingdom, that realm within you, is a place of peace. It can only be gained by love."[3]

"Imagine that waiting for God is like being a babe in arms, content to rest without squirm or scream in his mother's loving nearness!"

Even recognizing the necessity of stillness, it is extraordinarily difficult for many of us to practice it. Both outer and inner noise hinder us. The sheer volume of external noise and clutter around us can deafen us to the voice of God. Disturbance is everywhere. Phones and sirens, argument and chitchat, the roar of the crowd assail both ear and eye. Traffic bustles, tires squeal, brakes screech. The beeps, bells, and blasts of electronic gizmos assault us at every turn. For many, radio and television provide background noise from morning until night, even during meals. To this we add the noise of rushing through our own hectic schedules, noise that assails our senses and our spirits.

Though external noise often thwarts us in the struggle for stillness, our inner turmoil hinders us still more and even spawns many of our outer distractions. It is a witness to the spiritual poverty of our culture, for example, that in response to the question, "How are you?" we so often hear the answer, "I'm keeping busy," as if busyness were a guiding spiritual value or an adequate measure of our worth and achievement. Yet the false value of busyness governs many lives and smothers stillness. I find it embarrassingly difficult, for example, to sit still without picking up a book, taking up a task, or in some other way keeping busy. When I attempt to enjoy times of stillness, I find it far too easy to rate myself against colleagues and friends who are praised for productivity won through frenzied labor. Spiritual madness, I observe, *does* have its temporal rewards. Beside lust for activity spring up many other inner noises, including the appetite for material goods, self-doubt, the overbearing need for approval, worry, and other needs and desires that shout insistently within.

Even religious activity can become noise that inhibits the stillness of waiting. Many of us who would be devout seem not to believe that God is at work while we are at rest, for we give ourselves to such a relentless round of religious meetings and duties that stillness is impossible. Though such activities are helpful in their proper place, some of us, perhaps, should quit chasing after religious books, Bible studies, and noble works of

Christian service so that we can stand still to hear God's voice. Religious noise is noise all the same, and it can easily drown out the gentle, steady call of the Holy One. As Kenneth Leech wisely points out: "There is no need to rush around feverishly looking for a prayer life: we need to slow down and look deeply within. What is the point of complaining that God is absent if it is we who are absent from God, and from ourselves by our lack of awareness?"[4] A wise prioress once identified the same problem in saying, "Most books on religion have thousands of words—we need only one word, GOD—and that surrounded not by many words but by silence."[5]

"Religious activity is noise all the same, and it can easily drown out the gentle, steady call of the Holy One."

If we are to build serene inner spaces, we must learn to still the noises that would hinder us. A practical way to begin is to reduce the volume of outward noises, many of which we can control. Simply turn off the radio and television, for example, and use them only selectively, instead of as musical wallpaper. Establish periods of quietness in the home, in which the family forgoes conversation and noisy activity. Choose carefully the number and types of voices to which you will listen. An interest in the news, I have found, can easily become obsessive and destroy stillness. One antidote is to read and listen to the news less often. You don't need to hear every newscast in order to be informed. Similarly, don't submit to "news on the hour" headline broadcasts. Their breathless urgency too easily scatters the spirit and skews reality. Plan tasks and appointments so that you can move from one to another without needlessly creating inner hurriedness. By making simple choices like these, we can reduce noise in surprisingly helpful ways.

Even though we don't all control our schedules equally, we all can arrange them to build stillness. Certainly some duties will fall to anyone who has made a commitment to a job, family, church, or other group of people. However, in addition to the time duty requires, many of us feel invaded by an army of "demands" on our time. Friends, the church, the school, the family, the civic club, our special interests, and a hundred more each try to outshout the others as they bid for our energy and attention. In the midst of such a clamor of duty and demand, we must make choices for stillness. A first step is to recognize what, in fact, our duties are. Many of us saddle ourselves with obligations that are not ours and go far beyond what duty requires, often harming ourselves and others. Well-intentioned people who applaud such extra-mile devotion to duty make right choices even harder, but often they are barely aware (and hardly care) that our spirits are withering under the heat of our breakneck pace. Part of the value of waiting is that through it we can learn which duties are real and which are illusory.

We fool ourselves, though, when we simply blame others, for often it is our own weakness that upgrades requests to the status of "demands." Surely some people do pressure us, but more often we twist our own arms with our pride, our lust for activity, or our insatiable need to please others. The things we choose to do are, by and large, worthy enough, but we must learn that we can be tyrannized as easily by the good as by first-rate wickedness. If we are to establish stillness in our lives, then we will have to say no to some good things and to some nice people in order to have it. Ironically, it is waiting for God, which we so seriously jeopardize with calendars crammed full, that can help us learn what to take up and what to turn away.

"If we are to establish stillness in our lives, then we will have to say no to some good things and to some nice people in order to have it."

While we work to reduce the noise around us, we can also actively create places and times of stillness. For example, if we would put it on our calendars and guard it as jealously as any other appointment, many of us could arrange a day, a weekend, or even longer, for a personal retreat. Short of that, however, even little interludes of solitude can leaven the whole day. I find that five minutes of silence scheduled between appointments or before classes bring benefits completely out of proportion to the time spent. Better yet is the centering and stilling effect of taking fifteen minutes alone to stroll under the impressive arches of maples, elms, and cottonwoods. Even lingering quietly for a few extra minutes in the locker room, after playing racquetball, has often refreshed my sense of peace. Whether a week-long retreat to a mountain cabin or a five-minute recess in a bedroom or office, planned times of solitude feed the inner stillness, which can grow to permeate even the most active parts of our lives.

A time-tested way of coming to stillness is to learn the

disciplines of meditation and listening prayer (also called "contemplative prayer" and "meditative prayer"). These methods, based on silence and on the expectation that God will come to those who wait, are old and proven practices. The psalmists speak often of meditating, as in "meditating on the Law day and night," and urge practices similar to the historic practice of Christian meditation. For example, one singer advises, "When you are on your beds, search your hearts and be silent" (4:4, NIV), a phrase another modern translation renders "spend your night in quiet meditation." The point, of course, is not observing silence for its own sake, for there are many kinds of silence, but is instead shaping vigilant silences that build stillness.

The term *listening prayer* may be misleading in a way, for it incorrectly implies that it is possible to pray without listening. To approach God with only an incessant stream of words is a filibuster, not prayer. On the other hand, listening prayer, as Henri Nouwen points out, helps us learn how to wait:

> Contemplative prayer is not a way of being busy with God instead of with people, but it is an attitude in which we recognize God's ultimate priority by being useless in his presence, by standing in front of him without anything to show, to prove, or to argue, and by allowing him to enter into our emptiness. It is not useful or practical but a way of wasting time for God.[6]

Another of the classic spiritual disciplines that can help still our noisy hearts is fasting. By refraining for a time from food, from certain habits of buying and entertainment, or from other activities, we can break the cycle of false urgency and impulsiveness that would dominate us. Desire untamed would roam freely within us, roaring that we must meet its demands instantly.

Added to our own unruly desires is the constant barrage of advertising and even the influence of our friends, all of which conspire at times to transform whim to necessity and to make us crave things we had scarcely thought about before. By experimenting creatively with fasting we can address both our own weakness and the temptations that come to us. To see that we can skip one or more meals or that we have survived nicely without buying what we so desperately "needed," for example, shows up the lie of urgency for what it is. Physical acts of self-restraint, particularly coupled with prayer, help to purify our sense of need and to still the noise in our hearts.

Waiting for Strength

One of the striking facts in the Old Testament is how often the ideas of stillness and strength occur together. Probably the best-known passage is Isaiah 40:31 (author's translation): "Those who wait on the Lord will renew their strength. They will soar on wings like eagles; they will run and not grow weary, they will walk and not tire." But this connection is also made elsewhere in the Old Testament, particularly in Isaiah and in the Psalms. For example, Psalm 27:14 (NIV) counsels: "Wait for the Lord; be strong and take heart and wait for the Lord" (see also 31:24, 62:1, 7). The Old Testament stories, however, reveal that many of the Israelites, just like many of us, could hardly believe that the ideas of waiting and strength belong together. They often preferred that God bless their show of strength rather than be their source of strength. Because we share their doubt, we need to ask what it is about waiting that brings strength.

Waiting builds strength, in part, by moving us away from

deceptive self-reliance and toward dependence on God. In stillness we not only grant God freedom to act, but we also confess that we must sing, "The Lord is the strength of my life" (27:1, KJV). Dependence comes quite easily in times of emergency, of course, as when the Israelites were backed up against the sea, with the Egyptian chariotry bearing down on them. In that instance Moses told the terrified people, "The Lord will fight for you; you need only to be still" (Exodus 14:14, NIV). But when we are in less danger of being run over by enemy chariot wheels, many of us tend to rely on our own cunning and prowess to face everyday life, compounding the error of pride with a false estimate of our resources for living. Waiting wants to teach, in part, that God is more than an emergency kit to be broken open only after we have made a mess of life on our own. One common obstacle to admitting dependence is that we don't quite believe that God has our best interests and smallest needs at heart. We find it hard to imagine that the Eternal One would focus love on our little lives. Having created an illusory gap in God's care, it is easy to fall into self-sufficiency, using popular justifications like, "The Lord helps them that help themselves." Our eagerness for quick solutions in life also pushes us to rush ahead of God, rather than wait, trying to guarantee in our strength that everything will turn out all right. George Fox counsels that this is exactly backwards:

> Be still and cool in thy own mind and spirit from thy own thoughts, and then thou wilt feel the principle of God to turn thy mind to the Lord God, whereby thou wilt receive his strength and power from whence life comes, to allay all tempests, against blusterings and storms.[7]

In a broader way, waiting for God builds strength because in waiting we mature toward seeing life in truer perspective. "The contemplative is someone who sees things for what they really are," writes Henri Nouwen,[8] and it is precisely as we look through the lens of eternity and see reality for what it is that we are freed to live in a wholly new way. The psalmists warn, for example, not to trust or resent the apparent success of the evil rich (Psalms 37 and 73), for it ends in disaster. It is precisely this kind of purified vision that penetrated the lives of the Hebrew prophets. Because they knew God and saw through God's eyes, they knew the deceit around them even when their contemporaries did not. What Israel saw as right and proper worship, the prophets saw as blatant hypocrisy. What the wealthy saw as the blessing of God on their right-eousness, the prophets saw as damning evidence of theft, oppression, and twisted justice. Why? Because the prophets knew what was ultimate. They had met God face-to-face. Out of a perspective forged on the anvil of eternity, they could live, as we can, with uncommon courage and strength.

The power of the prophet's words in Isaiah 40, for example, grows out of this very perspective. His words of hope to a disheartened people reminded them that God is eternal, the Creator of the boundaries of the earth and the strengthener of the powerless. As the prophet declared, through waiting we can come to know God more truly as the Creator and Sustainer of life, as the only safe Shelter, as the One who is absolutely trustworthy, and as the One who constantly wraps our lives round with great tenderness, rather than as an ineffective, unreliable, distant deity. As we gaze steadily upon God in the stillness, we see the Holy One more genuinely than ever we could with occasional, hasty glances. Such a sharpening of our vision throws open the windows of our hearts so that the

Spirit of God may blow its refreshing breezes freely within us.

To encounter God in the stillness also helps us to see ourselves more clearly. Frankly, many of us avoid this, for the illusions that we hold about ourselves are the hardest to surrender. To see clearly is humbling and even frightening, for as Douglas Steere suggests, as the searchlight of reality shines on our lives, our petty self-justifications wither, and we are left face-to-face with our self-deceit and weakness.[9] We are embarrassed to see the missed opportunities and the repeated failures. We balk at discovering what God intends us to be, for this vision stands both as a judgment on our shortcomings and as a mandate to live in it in the future. Yet this is a bittersweet discovery, for we also see how wonderful God's purposes for us are. We begin to understand that God's vision for us far exceeds anything we can conceive, either in self-deprecation or in grandiose schemes. We come to know that we are loved beyond imagination and accepted in spite of soiled characters and puny souls. The love that comes to us in the stillness, as undeserved as it is, frees us to live only for God. It lifts the burden and deceit of grounding our self-worth on others' opinions of us or on society's artificial measurements of success and achievement. So waiting, as it allows us to see ourselves and God's care for us, frees us and gives us strength.

There is bold serenity in this kind of living. Maynard Shelley writes of the early Anabaptists, who advised in their tracts, "Let's be silent before Christ." Out of this silence emerged a quality of life they called *Gelassenheit*, a word variously translated "calmness of mind," "conquest of selfishness," "tranquillity," and "resignation." *Gelassenheit* prevailed dramatically in the rough-and-tumble of their living. One persecutor of the Anabaptists observed with disapproval that they "dance and jump into the flames, see the flashing sword without dismay, speak and preach to the spectators with laughing mouth; they sing psalms and hymns until their soul departs; they die with joy as if they were in a merry company; remaining strong, confident, and steadfast until their death." I am reminded of the early Quakers, thrown into stinking English prisons, who regarded their dungeons as castles, the locks as jewels, and sang boldly in praise, because they knew God would emerge victorious. Shelley remarks, "From such silence comes not just a spiritual experience but readiness to do God's will and to live with daring—daring to give to God the substance of their lives."[10] The willingness to risk encountering God in complete self-abandonment formed saintly lives and gave courage for their living. If we would live in the power of God, we, too, must wait.

Yielding Control

A persistent barrier to waiting is our reluctance to allow God to be completely in control. This should not surprise us at all, for it is the fundamental character of sin for us to want to be in charge of our own lives. We go to great lengths to assert our independence and to maintain mastery of a universe of our own creating. We even try to dictate the terms of our devotion to God. Yet waiting for God requires giving God complete freedom to act.

"God dwells only where man steps back to give him room," writes Henri Nouwen.[11] Waiting is giving God room. It cannot tolerate trying to drag God down out of the heavens on cue. It neither demands the encounter with God on our own terms nor expects that it will always be as it has been before— or as we have been told it must be. We must be willing to share the surprise of Elijah, who strained uselessly to hear God in the fiery, rock-shattering tempest, as Moses had, but who heard the divine voice out of the gentle stillness. Part of the risk of genuine devotion is that God may come to us in new ways, perhaps in subtle disguise ("When did we see you hungry?" the baffled self-righteous asked [*see* Matthew 25:31-46]) or in overwhelming power. To wait is to yield control.

Meister Eckhart speaks directly to this barrier to waiting:

> Aware of it or not, people have wanted to have the "great" experiences; they want it in this form, or they want that good thing; and this is nothing but self-will. Yield completely to God and then be satisfied, whatever he does with his own. . . . Indeed, one step taken in surrender to God is better than a journey across the ocean without it.[12]

"Waiting is giving God room. It cannot tolerate trying to drag God down out of the heavens on cue."

Yielding control, both necessary and difficult, is not simply a one-time choice, but a continuing discipline that can be learned. In specific acts of "resignation," we must consign to God's will and action all that we care about. We must specifically give over to God all the matters that we are eager to control and pray, "Thy will be done," a prayer Evelyn Underhill calls both "a prayer of pure realism" and "the prayer of docility."[13] Such radical resignation is found in the writings of Augustine Baker, a seventeenth-century English priest. In a long list of "acts of resignation," Baker renounces virtually everything: physical comfort, health, reputation, relationships, the character of his spiritual experience, his spiritual weakness, and much more. In one resolution he writes: "For Thy love, O my God, and in conformity to Thy holy will, I resign myself unto Thee, with all that I am, have, can do, or suffer, in soul, body, goods, fame, friends, etc., both for time and eternity."[14] As we learn to make such prayers of resignation our own, we also learn the yielding that makes waiting for God possible.

Another path to the surrender we need is to quit demanding control in our daily living. Picture the various situations or groups with which you want to have influence—the PTA, the church board, the task force on the job—and practice saying to yourself, *It's okay if things are not done my way. It's okay if I am not considered to be influential. I don't need to have impact.* We can subdue our imperialistic selves by choosing to be less aggressive and to initiate action less frequently in our contacts with others. Where we do take the initiative, we can scrutinize ourselves to see whether this action is under God's guidance or if it is proceeding instead out of our own willfulness and misguided need to feel important.

We can also infuse yieldedness into our lives by observing the Sabbath principle. The very essence of the Sabbath is to yield control and to delight instead in the rest of waiting and dependence. The Sabbath, writes Abraham Heschel, is a "realm of time where the goal is not to have but to be, not to own but to give, not to control but to share, not to subdue, but to be in accord."[15]

It is giving up our compulsiveness, our manipulation, our having to get the upper hand in our work or with our fellows. One of the great losses of the contemporary Christian community, both personally and corporately, is that the spirit of the Sabbath is almost entirely lacking. Forgetting that observing the Sabbath is something far more profound than merely going to church, many congregations pack their Sundays full of public meetings, committee meetings, and other activities, declaring participation in them a mark of true righteousness. In so doing they often foster an unholy intensity about doing the work of the Kingdom and a feverishness that wears us out rather than refreshes us, that feeds our compulsiveness rather than rebukes it. Individually, as well, we abuse the Sabbath principle in ways that go well beyond letting our work spill over into a day God has set apart for our joy and our good.

Churches could make a wonderful contribution in our stressful society if they would turn from apostasy in this matter and reshape their common lives to the spirit of the Sabbath. Short of that, however, we can learn individually the ways of the Sabbath without falling into harsh legalisms. We can plan our schedules in a way that will allow the joyful observance of a Sabbath each week. We can learn to lay down our work for a time, to celebrate the creation and one another, to rest and worship, and in many other ways, such as games, walks in the park, and festive meals, learn to rejoice in the providence and goodness of God. One of the wonderful bonuses of taking the Sabbath seriously is that we can soon learn to build little Sabbaths into our daily experience and, through this, learn more and more how to give up our need to control and how to yield up our lives to God.

We can also learn yieldedness through submitting ourselves to the authority of others. We balk at this, of course, in an intensely privatistic time, but it is this prevailing individualism, in religion as well as in society at large, that makes submission so important. To submit to the spiritual authority of others both confesses our need and recognizes that they can be channels of God's guidance and grace. I am not suggesting that we set ourselves under any casual gathering of religious folk, nor am I endorsing hierarchical authority. I am simply saying that there is immeasurable benefit in trusting oneself to a spiritual director or to a group characterized by spiritual maturity, discerning wisdom, and love rooted in God. Though other factors might prevent taking this step, pride and the need to maintain control most easily hinder us, and it is precisely for this reason that we should seriously consider submission as a steady discipline in the life of devotion. It is another way in which we learn to yield control so that we can come to know God.

Jean-Pierre de Caussade writes of a state of self-surrender in which at any moment, "the soul, light as a feather, fluid as water, innocent as a child, responds to every movement of grace like a floating balloon."[16] In just such a state, waiting for God can go forward in all of its expectancy, stillness, patience, and yieldedness. It is such an inner movement that allows us to be still and to know the reality of God.

THREE
TREMBLING

My whole being trembles before you,
your rulings fill me with fear.

Psalm 119:120

A lready by noon the day had become a twisted complex of meeting appointments, running errands, and fighting traffic. Even the bright prospect of a special lunch with my young daughter was clouded by the smog of my hectic morning. Between bites of fast-food chicken and nibbles of conversation, I looked out the window at the busy intersection nearby. Hannah gazed instead at the freshly green trees and the azure sky. "I just love being in God's wonderful world!" she declared abruptly. Her joyful innocence brought me up short. Though we talk freely about the life of faith in our family, in this instance she had seen God, and I, blinded by routine, had not. "Above the heavens is your majesty chanted by the mouths of children, babes in arms" (8:2).

The old spiritual "Were You There?" also searches me by asking not only whether I have seen but also what, having seen, my response will be. "Were you there when . . . ?" Have you seen it experientially?" is meddlesome enough, but the singer's response to having been there poses the most penetrating question. "Sometimes it causes me to tremble, tremble, tremble." A deep stillness and power and a glimpse into mystery rise out of those haunting lyrics. "Sometimes . . . to tremble." I seldom hear that phrase without wondering whether I have seen into the Mystery deeply enough to be moved by it and whether, if I have, I am vulnerable enough to tremble. The questions persist, I am sure, because to see and to be overcome in response are part of a growing inner life.

Though our modern sensibilities may resist it, trembling depicts an essential movement of the heart before God. In the Psalms, it describes the singers' response to powerful experiences of awe, wonder, and fear in the face of the overwhelming majesty of God. If we would understand their songs and, more important, nurture the inner life, we, too, must learn to tremble.

As important as it is, trembling, or the experience of awe, is largely absent from our ordinary living. One reason surely is that we are so desensitized by our own living that we are numb to seeing the holy. Our pace of life and highly managed environments, for example, can drown out even a thunderous divine voice. Movies, professional sports, and other entertainments add a numbing crescendo of contrived excitement that so confuses us that, in the end, truly wondrous experiences are demeaned as trite and the most trivial incidents elevated as "awesome," "tremendous," and "wonderful."

We also shrink from fearing God because we dare not fear the terror that lurks around us daily. So great is the scope of the threats to life—for example, global economic or environmental disaster and, most of all, our nuclear madness—that many of us try to escape fear by ignoring our inner lives almost completely. We are scared to death but not alive to fear, including a sense of wonder and fear toward God.

Sometimes our popular world view and social awareness also hinder experiences of awe. For example, many people, even religious folk, see at best a God who is distant and unlikely to be encountered significantly in the "real world." Some theologians have blamed the Bible for teaching this, arguing that it assumes a "three-story universe" in which God resides on the top floor, isolated from the world in which we live. Such interpreters are simply wrong. Although the biblical writers insist on the transcendence of God, they clearly do not confuse that with distance or inaccessibility. It is, instead, the prosaic and mechanistic spirit of our own age that presumes to shut God out and to predispose us not to expect experiences of awe.

"It seems odd that, while all creation shudders in dread before the power and purity of the Terrifying One, we should rest placidly, wholly untouched by his Presence."

A social barrier to a sense of awe is unmasked by how easily people shudder at the strong physical and emotional overtones of the phrase "trembling before God." For many it is simply not sophisticated to let religion touch them very deeply or very visibly. Physical trembling is not our main concern, of course, but I hesitate to put readers at ease too quickly on this point, for it seems odd that, while all creation shudders in dread before the power and purity of the Terrifying One, we should rest placidly, wholly untouched by his Presence.

We should, at least, recall that trembling or other physical responses to the Presence of God have often occurred throughout the history of faith. From Saul's attention-getting ecstasy and Belshazzar's knees clattering together, through Quaker and Wesleyan revivals, and on up to modern times, many report a bodily answering to the reality of God. Not only is such experience common, but it is also widely varied. Whether in rowdy dancing and goosebumps or in a deep, physically restful peace, the encounter with God has often prompted a physical response. Perhaps part of our own hesitancy about "trembling" may well be the fear that our responses to God may not be as prim and proper as we prefer.

To say that trembling before God has often been accompanied by such experiences is not the same, however, as prescribing that everyone should respond in the same way. Nonetheless, what we see more and more clearly today is that mind, body, psyche, and spirit are woven together so inseparably that we should expect to be affected as whole persons when we encounter God. Certainly we should see that the experience of God is not one of the mind alone or of a disembodied soul or spirit. Though physical responses can be (and often are) created artificially, they are, at their best, expressions of an authentic encounter, tokens of a profound trembling within.

It is this inner trembling that we must know, despite our numbness and resistance. In the Psalms, one of the words that most helpfully unfolds this experience to us is the word *fear.* God is described as one who elicits dread; individuals, nations, and nature are urged to fear God; and many, overwhelmed by God, are said to be filled with fear at God's presence or action. The language of fear is abundant, but it is also quite varied in tone. To fear God, in the Psalms, does not always mean quivering in anxiety or terror, but can also describe a profound sense of reverence or awe, though this is something far weightier than a childlike courtesy to the Cosmic Grownup. In some cases, fear refers to faithful ritual practice, particularly in passages referring to *God-fearers*. To see this variety of meanings should warn us against defining the "fear of God" too narrowly in terms of emotional or mystical experience.

"The temptation to shrink God to the size of our spirits constantly presents itself, even when we reject sentimentalism."

The heart of the experience of fear and trembling is to feel and acknowledge God over against us. God is the Wholly Other, the Mystery that comes to us but overreaches our comprehension and control, the crackling Power that steals our breath away. To encounter this Holy One leaves us awestruck, overcome by the Light, melted by unthinkable love. We may gasp within or be helplessly buoyed up in holy hilarity, with great waves of laughter filling and rolling out of every corner of our beings. Or the awe may strike us dumb with the silence of those who know too much, like the Apostle Paul who, caught up into Paradise, "heard things which must not and cannot be put into human language" (2 Corinthians 12:4). Most of us have had glimpses of the One beyond ourselves, though often in quieter, less dramatic ways. To tremble, however we may experience it, is to know the magnificent otherness of God.

Such trembling prevents our experience of God from proving in fact the common charge that God is merely our own creation, a religious or psychological extension of ourselves. Frankly, the temptation to shrink God to the size of our spirits constantly presents itself, even when we reject tawdry sentimentalism such as talk about "the Man Upstairs," "the Big Guy," and the like. It would be more to our liking to domesticate God a bit, to insist that the Most High conform to our tidy creeds and best-said prayers. But for this very reason we need to tremble. To be awestruck shatters such small-minded illusions.

The Psalms help us particularly at this point, for they are bursting with majestic, overwhelming images of God. Though some of them are slightly askew of modern sensibilities, these images can teach us and guide us to recover a lost sense of wonder. They can help to break the enchantment of confining views of reality so that we may awake and truly see God.

The Heavens Are Telling

One of the main witnesses to wonder in the Psalter is the created world itself:

> The heavens declare the glory of God,
> the vault of heaven proclaims his handiwork;
> day discourses of it to day,
> night to night hands on the knowledge.
> No utterance at all, no speech,
> no sound that anyone can hear;

yet their voice goes out through all the earth,
and their message to the ends of the world.

—Psalm 19:1-4

Theologians refer to creation's witness to God as *general revelation,* but it seems to me that this is too dull a term to describe the electricity of experience. Most of us remember moments, usually without theological labels, when the heavens were shouting God's glory, and it stopped us dead in our tracks. One such moment for me was a dazzling display of the aurora borealis over New Hampshire's Lake Winnipesaukee. At the sudden appearance of these "northern lights," I, along with other campers, craned my neck backward in wonder, but soon lay flat on my back to try to take in every nuance of light I possibly could. In ever-changing shades of blue, pink, and orange, the lights rolled and rippled, pulsing in waves, bursting in concentric circles of iridescence, shimmering in jeweled arcs across the sky. They left me breathless, caught somewhere between a whispered "WOW!" and no words at all. And I marveled at God.

Wonder again captured me in the moment of jaw-dropping awe when I first saw the Grand Tetons. These peaks in northwestern Wyoming are youthful, as mountains go, having tilted out of a high Rocky Mountain plateau only 10 million years ago. So they remain craggy and brawny with the sharp edges of their youth still to be worn off. My memory says we came on them suddenly, or so it seemed, driving around a bend to meet their lofty stare. Open-mouthed and speechless at their alpine splendor, again I marveled at God.

Creation declares the glory of God to us in myriad ways, and we each hear its voice differently. The voice may come through surging rivers or crashing seas, through the intricate beauty of a rose or the delicacy of a dandelion gone to seed, through the soaring majesty of an eagle or the bouncing flight of the goldfinch; it may come through scowling gray-green thunderheads or through a flaming pink sunset sky. Whatever the source, the silent voice addresses us and comes to help us tremble in eager amazement before the Creator.

In the Psalms the creation tells us of God in two ways: through its own response to God and through its witness to others. One of the most remarkable and persistent images in all of the Old Testament as well as in the Psalms is how readily nature itself responds to the presence and activity of God. At a touch the mountains smoke (144:5), and they "melt like wax at the coming of the Master of the world" (97:5). When Yahweh reigns as king, the earth quakes (99:1), and when the divine verdict thunders down from heaven, the earth "stays silent with dread" (76:8). The powerful voice of Yahweh "sets the wilderness shaking"; it shatters the cedars of Lebanon and makes mountains leap like calves and young wild bulls (29:5-6). It causes great waters to turn back with a shudder (77:16) and flee to their appointed places (104:7-9). In these and many other ways, all creation trembles in fear or bursts with vitality at the presence of the Giver of Life.

Similarly, nature joins in praise and gladly tells of God's wonders throughout the world. The creation witnesses to God's inventiveness, wisdom, and tender care. "Your miracles," sings the psalmist, "bring shouts of joy to the portals of morning and evening" (65:8). And all creatures seem eager to answer the call to laud the glory and goodness of God (for example, see Psalm 148 and many other places).

Though the Hebrew singers, I suspect, were moved by the witness of nature more readily than we are, we can learn to listen more deeply as a way of nurturing trembling in our own hearts. A first step is to break down the wall between ourselves and creation. We almost universally consider the world to be mere matter, a mechanical contrivance assembled from objective, impersonal particles of stuff. Handicapped by such a view, we can hardly picture the trees clapping their hands and the hills skipping like lambs in response to God, even though we may admire the wonderfully poetic quality of these images. It is hard for us to imagine creation responding to God in any way except as a machine. Perhaps new directions in physics and other sciences will turn us away from this longstanding, mechanistic view, but in any event, people of faith can learn to take seriously the clear biblical teaching that nature, like us, does respond to God, for in doing so we can be drawn to see more clearly the power and intimacy of God's rule.

Another step toward receiving the witness of nature is to recover our sense of God as Creator. Tragically, in our time, even people of faith have had their sense of God as Creator diminished and even destroyed, not only by the scientists who go beyond science to make theological pronouncements, but also by interpreters of the Bible who impoverish biblical teaching on creation through needlessly narrow readings of the text. Even those who have not enlisted on one side or the other of the Bible-versus-science war have often been robbed of the liveliness of the majestic images of God's creative power. Fortunately, we can reclaim what has been stolen away. Rather than insisting that the Bible answer the inappropriate questions our century would put to it, we can hear the Bible on its own terms. We can, instead, open our hearts to the powerful and varied word pictures that show God speaking the world into being, becoming a sculptor and surgeon, spreading out the heavens like a tent, measuring the seas in the palm of his hand, weighing the mountains in balance scales, and much more. To know inwardly the whole of biblical teaching about God as Creator can help to renew our sense of awe.

We can also hear the heavens declare God's glory simply by paying more attention to nature and learning to cherish its marvels. Whether through avocation or disciplined scientific study, such familiarity can point us to God. My family enjoys bird-watching both at home and as we travel, and we hear constantly through this of the inventiveness and even the play-fulness of God. A friend of mine tells eagerly of how his insatiable reading about astronomy and other sciences increases his wonder at God. Others of us hear the same witness through gardening, camping, backpacking, and in many other ways. All creation does tell of the glory of God, and we will advance in our spiritual journey if we will listen. "Earth's crammed with heaven, And every common bush afire with God; But only he who sees, takes off his shoes," wrote Elizabeth Barrett Browning.[1] We can learn to see so that we may take off our shoes.

Wonders of Power and Love

Perhaps we most readily connect trembling and awe with being overwhelmed by an ominous power or presence. True to our expectations, the Psalms do include many examples of fear prompted by God's power. What is particularly striking in the Psalms, however, is how often the experience of trembling before God is evoked not by power, but by overwhelming love. Christian hymnody has continued this pervasive Psalms theme. In his great hymn, for example, Reginald Heber writes, "Holy, holy, holy, Merciful and Mighty . . . Perfect in power, in love, and purity."[2] Robert Grant expresses the same truth beautifully as he addresses God as "Our Maker, Defender, Redeemer and Friend."[3] We come to stand in awe, then, at the wonders of power and love.

The images of power are potent and plentiful. The fact of creation establishes God's unrivaled authority. God as "the Great King of the whole world" is to be dreaded (47:2), and causes the nations to tremble and the earth to shake (99:1). The Lord is feared for the powerful acts of deliverance, the "terrible deeds," in Israel's history, most notably the Exodus from Egypt (*see* 66:1-6). God's judgment on the wicked produces fear in all humankind (64:9), including the righteous (52:6). Even the holiness of God occasions dread (99:14; 111:9). Throughout the Psalms the singers recount Yahweh's glory, splendor, majesty, incomparability, and power.

Among these wonders of power, however, are also the wonders of love. The Creator of the world rules also as its Sustainer, whose "tenderness embraces all his creatures" and who "feeds them all with a generous hand" (145:9, 16; *see also* 104:27-30).

No despot, this benevolent Monarch refuses to wield power maliciously or capriciously, but compelled by love, uses it to protect and prosper the people. Even the sharp verdicts against the wicked grow out of grace, for they are rendered to further the fulfillment of the people's (and God's) desires for justice and peace. The foreboding holiness of God, too, is anchored in love as the faithful are invited to be like God in holiness (Leviticus 19:2) and as they experience forgiveness. "If you never overlooked our sins, Yahweh, Lord, could anyone survive?" the ancient singers asked. "But you do forgive us: and for that we revere [fear] you" (130:3-4).

Steeped in the Psalms, Isaac Watts captured how grace penetrates power when he wrote, "He rules the world with truth and grace, And makes the nations prove The glories of His righteousness, And wonders of His love."[4] When we combine our visions of God's majesty and of God's love, we move even more directly toward awe and adoration. Thomas Merton describes this experience beautifully:

> When one becomes conscious of who God really is, and when one realizes that He who is Almighty, and infinitely Holy, has "done great things to us," the only possible reaction is the cry of half-articulate exultation that bursts from the depths of our being in amazement at the tremendous, inexplicable goodness of God to men.[5]

When our eyes are opened to see that the Power of the universe is steadily focused toward us in love, we can scarcely do anything else but tremble.

How Can It Be?

The great tension between the majestic otherness and the tender intimacy of God reaches its peak as we consider what our own lives mean and what it means to be human. Those questions often come forcefully to me on those brilliantly starry nights when I seem to myself little more than a miniscule speck in an incomprehensibly vast universe. With the questions often come the lyrics of Psalm 8. I share their question and am helped by their answer:

> *I look up at your heavens, made by your fingers,*
> *at the moon and stars you set in place—*
> *ah, what is man that you should spare a thought for him,*
> *the son of man that you should care for him?*
> *Yet you have made him little less than a god,*
> *you have crowned him with glory and splendour. . . .*

—Psalm 8:3-5

It should hardly surprise us that the question of our worth often comes so freshly. Even more dramatically than the psalmist, I am sure, we are overwhelmed by the sheer dimension of the universe. It is mind-boggling to imagine that each of us is only one of nearly 4 billion people on a little planet circling an undersized sun among more than 200 billion others in the Milky Way, which, again, is only one galaxy of 100 billion more. Our sense of insignificance seems to grow whenever the scope of problems even on our planet seems too vast for us, whether they be environmental, social, or political. We are reminded, too, of how fragile and transitory life itself is every time we suffer the loss of someone dear to us. At another point where the psalmists asked, "What is man?" their question was based on this reality. "Man's life, a mere puff of wind," they said, "his days, as fugitive as shadows" (144:4). It is no surprise, then, that we should puzzle over our own significance.

At the very least, the weight of such questions and perceptions surely should persuade us that we, who are tiny pinpoints in space and time, can hardly rival the Eternal Creator. This alone should prompt us to take up the refrain, "Sometimes it causes me to tremble." But to be overwhelmed by sheer dimension and power falls far short of the wonder of the psalmists. They are even more amazed at God's love. Sören Kierkegaard reflects their spirit in one of his prayers: "God in Heaven, let me really feel my nothingness, not in order to despair over it, but in order to feel the more powerfully the greatness of Thy goodness."[6]

In the midst of the psalmist's sense of nothingness, we see something else quite remarkable. "Yet you have made him little less than a god," he writes. Though traditional translations read here "lower than the angels," the phrase can as readily be translated "little less than God" (8:5, RSV). Not only is this linguistically correct, but it also agrees with the creation account of Genesis 1, which declares that humankind was made in the "image of God." This teaching goes well beyond refuting the idea that man is simply a biochemical accident that has happened into the world. It calls us, instead, to see in our humanity reflections of the very character of God, including, at least, personhood, the capacity for love and relationship, freedom, creative power, a gracious authority over the created order, and much more. From the point of view of the biblical writers, to be made "little less than God" witnesses to the stunning goodness of the Creator. What a marvel it is to think that our own existence and character flow out of a surfeit of divine love!

We should take care to avoid two common errors at this point. The first is to fall into an arrogantly confident assessment of human capacity, an error particularly common in our time. There is a widespread sense of human self-sufficiency, a sense that we can conquer anything (even, in some sense, death) if we simply have enough time. Rather than being led into false confidence and blind ingratitude, when we see human creativity, skill, and power, we should come to rejoice again in God, in whose likeness we have been made. On the other hand, we must not imagine that our likeness to God has been obliterated or removed because of human wickedness. Indeed, the only reason humans can be so bad is because they are so good. The corruption of creative power has given us the gas chambers of Auschwitz and the nuclear incineration of Hiroshima and Nagasaki. A twisting of our trusteeship over the world has brought wholesale destruction to the environment. A perversion of the capacity to love has produced hollow, ruinous relationships. In the end, we must avoid the errors of both confidence and pessimism if we are fully to appreciate the goodness of God in choosing that we should share the divine image.

The fact that God has shown such care for humankind should, in itself, bring wonder. But we can also nurture our sense of awe by rejoicing in the reflection of God in the best of the human enterprise. Some people, for example, are brought to tremble before God as they admire the creative genius in a magnificent symphony or in an unusually inventive jazz improvisation. Others marvel at God as much as at ourselves for learning how to travel in space or perform a delicate heart surgery. Even more awe-inspiring to me are lives like those of Francis of Assisi, John Woolman, Dietrich Bonhoeffer, and Mother Teresa, lives so radiant that they reflect God's glory. Perhaps all of us have known persons who lived with such authentic power and love that we have been awestruck—amazed at them, but even more amazed at God. We have seen and been overcome by the image of the Creator in the creature.

"How can it be that we are invited not only to reveal the character of God, but also to share in it and even to have it born and brought to maturity in us?"

In the Christian faith, the most telling witness to the glory of God among men was in Jesus Christ. The Eternal Word became human, writes John. "He lived among us, and we saw his glory, the glory that is his as the only Son of the Father, full of grace and truth" (John 1:14). It is a remarkable life, one that dignifies humanity and points toward its God-given possibilities, one that has stirred wonder and admiration from all who learn of it. What is equally remarkable is that Jesus calls his disciples to share that kind of living. They are to live in a way that will cause people to glorify God (Matthew 5:16). They are to shine so brilliantly as children of light that they reflect like mirrors the radiant glory of God (2 Corinthians 3:18). How can it be, we may well ask, that we are invited not only to reveal the character of God, but also to share in it and even to have it born and brought to maturity in us? Often it causes me to tremble.

The Pure Heart

Perhaps the picture that can most readily cause us to tremble is a vision of the holiness of God. This is what overwhelmed Isaiah as he heard the seraphs calling out to one another, "Holy, holy, holy is Yahweh Sabaoth. His glory fills the whole earth" (Isaiah 6:3). A vision of God's holiness, along with an overwhelming sense of divine sovereignty, is at the heart of the foreboding Calvinist understanding of God. And it is the holiness of God, which Rudolf Otto associated with the *mysterium tremendum*, that can bring us to awe.

The idea of holiness in the Old Testament points toward purity and perfection. It refers to what is set apart from the common and the polluted, for the holiness of God cannot tolerate sin, the distorted or blemished, or the partial. So Hebrew religious practices required that worshipers should observe purification rituals and that objects used in worship should be unblemished and pure, whether they be garments or sacrificial animals. Holiness can be seen as the very essence of the character of God. It embraces and fuses all that we know about God. I see the holiness of God as an astonishingly pure, white light, one that we can hardly bear to see, but that is refracted to us through the prism of God's words and deeds. So what we see as divine love, justice, wrath, faithfulness, patience, and wisdom are simply beautifully refracted rays of the holiness of God. To see this holiness, whether through the prism's rainbow or directly in its dazzling purity, brings us to awe and worship. "Worship the Lord in the splendor of his holiness," sing the psalmists, "tremble before him, all the earth" (96:9, NIV).

Another expression of our trembling before God's holiness is repentance, for the contrast between what we see of God and what we know of our own lives is overwhelming. The pure light of God penetrates every corner of our own darkness and reveals every fleeting shadow. When we truly see the Holy One, we know instantly that Isaiah was right, and we cry out with him, "Woe is me!" (Isaiah 6:5, KJV). Yet even as the vision condemns us, it also draws us. We come to desire a pure heart. We desire to fulfill the call, "Be holy, for I, Yahweh your God, am holy" (*see* Leviticus 11:45). We yearn to be set apart for God, living in the world, but not sharing its corruption. The vision of holiness brings us to a repentance filled both with remorse and eager for transformation.

In the Psalms, we see three significant responses to the ideal of the pure heart. The first response surprises and annoys many of us. It is the poet's claim that he already has a pure heart. For example, one of the singers tells God, "You probe my heart, . . . you test me yet find nothing, . . . my mouth has never sinned as most men's do" (17:3-4). "What arrogant nerve!" we object, ready to join in the lyrics of Job's accusing friends. However, there is value in this claim, for it reminds us that God not only calls us to purity, but has also made it possible to achieve it. The facts of forgiveness and transformation are fundamental to both the Old and New Testaments.

A second response to the ideal of a pure heart seems more in keeping with a vision of the holiness of God. It is the sense of being overwhelmed by one's own sin. "My sins close in on me until I can hardly see, they outnumber the hairs on my head," despairs one singer (40:12). Another is so overcome by the depth of his sinfulness that he confesses in a moving hyperbole that it reaches even to the moment of his conception (51:5). Indeed, it seems impossible that anyone should be able to be judged righteous before God (143:2; 130:3). It is right that our comprehension of God should bring us to this kind of self-understanding and repentance. William Temple saw this clearly:

> If a man should claim to have had a vision of God which did not bring him to penitence, I should feel very sure that he had had no real vision, or that it was not a vision of the real God.[7]

It is striking how often the "saints," as we would measure them, seem to be deeply aware of their own sinfulness. I am sure, for example, that the repentant author of Psalm 51 (traditionally thought to be David) was an uncommonly righteous person. In the New Testament, Paul refers to himself as "the greatest of sinners" (see 1 Timothy 1:15). Similarly, the story is told of the great monk Abba Dioscurus that one of his disciples once chided him for weeping over his sins. "Truly, my child," Dioscurus is said to have replied, "if I were allowed to see my sins, three or four men would not be enough to weep for them."[8] It is no accident that the saints, who have seen God most truly, feel the weight of their sin most deeply. They were, as we must be, overwhelmed by the holiness of God.

"It is no accident that the saints, who have seen God most truly, feel the weight of their sin most deeply. They were, as we must be, overwhelmed by the holiness of God."

The Psalms provide yet a third response to the ideal of a pure heart, a way that mediates between confidence and contrition. Rather than answering, "I have one," or, "Mine's a rotten one," when we question whether we have a pure heart, we can respond, "I want one." In several key passages the psalmists show us the way of continuing confession and constant submission. They invite God to keep on with the work of transformation, of creating within them the holiness they so much desire. The psalmist who had at first complained that he couldn't escape God's close scrutiny, for example, comes round to conclude his song with this invitation:

> *God, examine me and know my heart,*
> *probe me and know my thoughts;*
> *make sure I do not follow pernicious ways,*
> *and guide me in the way that is everlasting.*

> —Psalm 139:23-24

Perhaps the Psalms' refrain that can most readily become a continual prayer is: "God, create a clean heart in me, put into

77

me a new and constant spirit" (51:10). By following this way of steady confession and submission, we can soon find that we not only are awed by God's holiness, but that we assent to it and are drawn by it and tremble in love before it, as we long to have the Holy One transform our lives.

F O U R

DESPAIRING

My God, my God, why have you deserted me?
I call all day, my God, but you never answer,
all night long I call and cannot rest.

Psalm 22:1-2

any seminarians go to school so they can learn to lead others in the life of faith. Not Frank. He was in seminary desperately trying to salvage a few shreds of faith for himself. He had become a Christian as a young adolescent, and his warm piety had eventually led him to serve the poor in a nation bordering on war. His own government had proclaimed its peaceful intentions there, but he soon learned its gunships routinely destroyed peasant villages and farmlands nearby. Frank's angry disbelief was galvanized into rage and despair when bombs fell on *campesinos* with whom he worked and he saw for himself women and children fleeing in terror, many with gaping wounds, all pierced to the heart. *Why?! Why does this happen? Why does God permit this?* The questions so burned themselves on his heart and shattered his faith that he could scarcely hear an answer, though he earnestly wanted to. His struggle for faith was overwhelmed by despair.

Less dramatic but more common is Stephanie's story. Though raised in the church, not until she was a young adult did Stephanie come into a faith that sparkled with life. The first weeks and months of discovery were a time of adventure and excitement. Energy and joy spilled over on everyone around her (often to their envy), and Stephanie thought her spiritual high tide would last forever. It didn't. Though she scrupulously tended her new life, periods of time came when prayer was difficult, devotion was more duty than delight, and life seemed more ordinary than thrilling. She, like many of us, was tempted to indict herself for spiritual sloth, to conclude that the sparkle maybe had been too good to be true, and to lower her hopes—or abandon them altogether. She struggled in faith, wondering about its meaning and its possibilities.

Frank and Stephanie's stories are not unusual. Even after longing for God and finally coming into faith, many people struggle, even to the point of despair. Though despair is almost too strong a word here, since it signifies the loss of hope, still it points accurately to the depth of distress that is possible for even the faithful. The struggles for faith are not mere trifles or charades. They sometimes jar us to the core.

Many modern teachers gloss over this reality. From the Cathedral of the Perpetual Smile to First Happy Baptist, there are plenty of people who would mistakenly have us believe that the life of faith is basically one long joyride. To sustain this illusion and the quest for the Holy Grin, they transform the church program into a religious amusement park hawking a thrill-a-minute, fun-filled experience, complete with emotional roller coasters, religious variety shows, verbal trick mirrors, and more. Such teaching is a half-truth at best, a shoddy imitation of authentic joy in faith. Both the Scriptures and our experience refute it.

The fact is that the life of faith includes struggle. We suffer dryness and "the dark night of the soul." We hear the piercing question, "Why?" and blush at not having a tidy answer. We cringe and cry out when life seems hollow and unfair. We smart under the sting of mockery and lies aimed at us. We sometimes plead, "My God, my God, why have you forsaken me?"

But even when we see the struggle in ourselves, we are tempted to conceal rather than disclose it. Sometimes we even put on our brave face before God. After all, to admit struggle seems to be admitting that we have failed as disciples. So while we feign joy, we trudge on, silently stooped by our burdens, and we secretly waste away. What we need to do, instead, is to unmask our struggle and despair and to learn, as people of faith, how to encounter them.

"Sometimes we even put on our brave face before God. After all, to admit struggle seems to be admitting that we have failed as disciples."

At this point the Psalms are a helpful guide, for songs of struggle—the laments—are the most common type of song in the Psalter. The Hebrew singers often sang "the blues," and the way they did it can teach us about our own times of darkness and how to open them to the light.

Though old and sometimes shrill, the lament songs still echo the themes of our despair. We hear in them our insistent question, "Why, if God is good, does life often seem unfair?" They sing of our bewilderment and anger over people who lie to us, gossip about us, and even try to ruin us. Even the melancholy strains of abandonment and loneliness come alive to us, for sometimes the psalmists, too, felt God mysteriously absent from them. The perennial question, "Why?" Enemies. The apparent absence of God. Though times may change, the lyrics of lament are timeless.

Water Up to My Neck

These Psalms surprise us, often, in how deeply the singers feel their distress. Even granting the exaggeration typical of Hebrew poetry, their pain leaps out at us. "I am worn out with groaning," writes one, "every night I drench my pillow and soak my bed with tears; my eye is wasted with grief" (6:6-7). Another sings of being exhausted from misery, "How much longer," he asks, "must I endure grief in my soul, and sorrow in my heart by day and by night?" (13:2). These troubles have aged them beyond their years (6:7). Of course, we need not hear such complaints merely as grand hyperbole. At this point we should not be surprised. Don't we know, too, what it means to be so careworn that we toss restlessly on our beds, vainly trying every method we know to get to sleep? Don't we know what it means to lose our appetites or to hesitate to go out in public for fear that we might at any moment break into tears? Sallow faces and vacant stares, the fruit of despair, are not far from any of us. Few of us have escaped being robbed of energy and a measure of life itself because of betrayal, grief, and other struggles of the soul.

Several of the psalmists are so burdened that they see

themselves teetering on the brink of death itself. They complain, for example, that they are being overwhelmed by the chaotic primordial waters, the waters through which one passed into the realm of the dead. Death threatens imminently when the singer cries out, "Save me, God! The water is already up to my neck! . . . I have stepped into deep water and the waves are washing over me" (69:1-2). This and other Old Testament allusions to rescue from the waters often portray a sense of impending death.

One Psalm links this picture specifically with the most common Old Testament image of death, Sheol, the world of the dead:

> For the waves of death encompassed me;
> The torrents of destruction overwhelmed me;
> The cords of Sheol surrounded me;
> The snares of death confronted me.

> —2 Samuel 22:5-6; Psalm 18:4-5, NASB

From the dim and dusty precincts of Sheol, in which all the dead reside, one neither returns nor praises the Almighty (as the despairing psalmists eagerly point out to God). Often, then, the singers cry out for rescue from their struggle as they see their lives "on the brink of Sheol" (88:3).

For the psalmists, death does not merely end life. It also invades our living and steals away its vigor. So when the psalmists cry, "The water is already up to my neck!" it is not just primitive hysteria. Instead, it describes graphically how deeply spiritual struggle can reach us. We are coming to understand this again as we see ever more clearly the interplay between body, mind, soul, spirit, psyche, or whatever other components into which we are prone to compartmentalize ourselves. Now we know, for example, that stress causes sickness. We see that in response to spiritual and psychological torment, our bodies often fashion diseases precisely to answer and express our pain, even to the point of death. I have seen a person develop a strong physical allergy to a place she detested and a young man fall victim to a crippling disease born of his own rage. We are told that grief can trigger cancer. Stress can ruin our hearts. In brief, spiritual struggle can have powerful, even physical, effects on our lives. It can be, literally, sickness unto death.

The Timeless "Why?"

"Why?" is not only one of the most persistent questions in the lament songs, it is one of the most urgent questions of all humankind. Fueled by visions of fairness, justice, and the power of God, "Why?" expresses our deep uneasiness and even open anger that the world is out of whack, that things are not as they are supposed to be.

One of the glaring inequities the psalmists see is that they suffer though they are innocent. In Psalm 44, for example, the singer expresses this very directly when he bemoans the defeat and disgrace into which his people have fallen:

> All this happened to us though we had not forgotten you,
> though we had not been disloyal to your covenant;
> though our hearts had not turned away. . . .
> Wake up, Lord! Why are you asleep? . . .
> Why do you hide your face,
> and forget we are wretched and exploited?

—Psalm 44:17-18, 23-24

Elsewhere, when the psalmists base a plea for deliverance on innocence, the question "Why?" surely is not far from the surface. "Why hold back your hand?" (74:11). "Why have you deserted me?" (22:1). "Why do you forget me? Why must I walk so mournfully, oppressed by the enemy?" (42:9; 43:2). "Why do you reject me?" (88:14).

Job, the classic case of the innocent sufferer, pushes this point to its limit. In his final defense speech (Job 29–31), Job details his innocence so thoroughly he makes even his sympathizers blush for him; then he ends with a flourish: If I can ever get a fair hearing with God, he says, "I will give him an account of every step of my life, and go as boldly as a prince to meet him" (Job 31:37). In Job's story, the question "Why?" is written in huge letters as a background to every page.

It is bad enough to suffer innocently, but it adds even further frustration and puzzlement to see scoundrels prosper. The singer in Psalm 73 complains that though the wicked are arrogant, powerful, violent, and insolent toward God, yet they have bodies that would be the pride of a health club, they have no pain, and they are making money hand over fist— they are "well-off and still getting richer!" (73:12). Such apparent inequity baffles and tempts the psalmist:

> *After all, why should I keep my own heart pure,*
> *and wash my hands in innocence,*
> *if you plague me all day long*
> *and discipline me every morning?*

—Psalm 73:13-14

The psalmists felt keenly the questions that thrust themselves on us each day. Some of them come to us from our televisions and newspapers. Why so much bad news? Why are people, even in the name of God, constantly at war? Why must many thousands of children each day starve to death, while their rich counterparts pay dearly to slim down at diet camps? Why do world leaders so often exude cold arrogance and greed? Some of our questions come from the neighborhood of our lives. Why is a young mother like Sally stricken with leukemia? How can his boss get away with firing someone as good as Jim? Why does Bob abuse his kids?

Many of our questions "Why?" however, don't force themselves on us from the outside, but erupt out of our own molten cores. *Why doesn't it seem to make more difference that I'm alive? Why, if God is with me, do I fail so often? Why, when I've done my best, is everything going wrong? Why bother? Why?*

One of the psalmists came near despair in answering his question:

> *Has God forgotten to show mercy,*
> *or has his anger overcome his tenderness?*

> *"This," I said then, "is what distresses me:*
> *that the power of the Most High is no longer what it was."*

> —Psalm 77:9-10

Perhaps God isn't loving. Perhaps God isn't powerful. Such bewilderment illustrates, I think, that the anguish of such questions may be even greater for people of faith than for others. Because we hope in a God who intends that the world should be just and who is loving and powerful, we have an agony over the dissonance between the way things are and the way they are supposed to be, to which the nonbeliever has no claim. Because of faith, the question "Why?" can become a crisis. So rather than deny the power and poignancy of our questions, we must admit their reality and their legitimacy. We do struggle and even despair, and as I will suggest, acknowledging that can be a first step toward rescue when the "water is up to our necks."

"Because we hope in a God who intends that the world should be just and who is loving and powerful, we have an agony over the dissonance between the way things are and the ways things are supposed to be."

Dogs and Lions

Not only do the psalmists struggle with "Why?" they also are unnerved in the face of their enemies, attackers who, by the singers' account, are bigger than life and twice as mean. The theme of "enemies" is one of the most frequent in the Psalms, but it is also one that proves troublesome to modern readers. Despite its difficulty, however, the "enemies" language can teach us, for it is about people we know and live with. It is about critics and detractors, about cheats and liars, about double-crossers who don't say what they mean and don't mean what they say. The psalmists' enemies are like people we meet every day.

We shouldn't be surprised or offended that the psalmists have enemies. The singers haven't sought them and don't seem to delight in the fact that others are out to get them. Frankly, enemies are a part of real life. Though it makes nice funeral rhetoric to say of the deceased, "He didn't have an enemy in the world," it's rarely true. From the prophets to Jesus, and to our own time, it is clear that people who serve God faithfully will have enemies. So will nearly everyone else.

The psalmists, however, claim to have premium-quality enemies, a horde of people despicable enough to stock a soap opera. They lie constantly and cheat. They are smooth talkers whose tongues are razor sharp and full of poisonous venom (52:2; 55:21; 64:3; 140:3). They are treacherous and cunning people, whose persuasive words hide the war in their hearts. They twist the psalmists' words, spy on them (56:5-6), set traps for them, pay back evil for kindness (109:5), and hate peace. They are like a pack of vicious dogs or a lion with fangs bared, eager to tear their victim limb from limb (22:13, 16, 20-21; 57:4). They're so bad that they "prefer evil to good, lying to honest speech" (52:3). Worst of all, they actually think they can get away with it. Over and over again the psalmists complain that the enemies believe that God ignores their wickedness or that he cannot or will not act to disrupt their schemes. While the struggling psalmists began to doubt whether God would act, their enemies had already decided that they were perfectly safe.

Although each of the psalmists' enemies qualifies easily as a candidate for the Villains' Hall of Fame, we can't tell exactly who they are. The psalmists don't name them, and they use bombastic clichés to describe them. Yet we should guard against merely spiritualizing or generalizing the enemy. To the Hebrew singers, the enemies were not distant or cerebral.

Certainly the psalmists knew of spiritual warfare, but they generally describe a distinctly flesh-and-blood conflict. Their life, goods, and reputation were at stake, and to make it worse, sometimes God didn't even seem to care. To see the enemies as a general category holds them at arm's length and discounts the power of the psalmists' experience. The first singers, at least (and many since them), have known their enemies personally.

Just like the psalmists, we know enemies are real. Though we may not use the same exaggerated language as they did, the words we do use of our enemies are often as intemperate and sometimes more inelegant than theirs. We, like the psalmists, are hurt and dismayed. Who among us has not been lied to and cheated by people we trust? Haven't we all been under the eagle eye of someone eager to broadcast our slightest error in ridicule and gossip? Some of us have had our bosses scheme to get rid of us. Others have been maligned by the envious and fearful. All of us at some point have been taken advantage of, lied about, smiled at by backstabbers, and much more. Sadly, the villainy of such "enemies" is universal. It even thrives in the community of faith. What makes this situation worse for the psalmists and for us is that we not only seem helpless in the face of our enemies, but we sometimes wonder whether our Divine Helper will rescue us in time. The real sticking point is not just that we have enemies, but that they often appear to have license to do whatever they please. In this we share with the psalmists the struggle of faith.

Vengeance and Babies' Heads

Many who are offended at the enemy language of the Psalms are troubled most by the "curses" some of the singers seem to hurl at their enemies. To wish that schemers would fall victim to their own traps seems just enough, but frankly, some of the "curses" are bitter and even brutal. One can understand, certainly, how a singer who had seen the Babylonians cruelly destroy his nation might wish that his oppressors' babies have their heads bashed against the rocks (137:9). But this is excessive in the larger context of both the Old and New Testaments. Certainly the Psalms talk about "hating" enemies, though even this terminology may have had a more technical or restricted sense than we see in it. On the other hand, the Old Testament clearly sees that vengeance belongs to God (Deuteronomy 32:35) and advises people to feed hungry enemies (Proverbs 25:21-22), counsel that Paul quotes with approval to the Christians in Rome (Romans 12:19-20). Careful study reveals that the cursing language is neither as vindictive nor as pervasive as it first appears, yet honesty compels us still to acknowledge (and perhaps to be troubled by) its presence. Before we wallow in self-righteousness, however, we ought to recognize, as C.S. Lewis and others have pointed out, that though these curses may not be a model for our behavior, they may well be a mirror.[1] Our own angry desires to get even may also well exceed the boundaries of both justice and compassion.

We must also see the psalmists' plea for "vengeance" in the context of their desire for God's just rule. The Hebrews did not view God as a cosmic hit man out to settle a score for them at their whim. Instead, they saw Yahweh as a sovereign ruler eager to establish peace and justice throughout the world. *Vengeance in the Old Testament is a function of God's just and righteous rule.* It has nothing to do with fits of temper or holding a grudge, traits we rightly see as unworthy of God. Vengeance is redressing wrong. It is delivering the oppressed. It is calling criminals to account and effecting the wise and compassionate rule that the whole creation welcomes with joy (Psalms 96; 98). And it is God's, not man's, business.

That is why the psalmists neither take vengeance (or justice) into their own hands nor curse their enemies directly. Instead, when they complain about the injustice they suffer, they appeal to God, whose right and obligation it is to see that justice is done. Even bitter complaints about the enemy are finally left in the hands of God.

In leaving vengeance to God, the psalmists teach us that even the most perplexing points of our struggle and despair must stand under God's sovereign wisdom. When our enemies prevail, life is unfair, justice is not done, and the Kingdom is clearly not established, we must choose to affirm, even through our complaint, "that tho the wrong seems oft so strong God is the Ruler yet."[2]

Even though this is sound teaching, the New Testament tells us that justice isn't good enough. The Psalms move us from personal revenge to justice, but Jesus moves us from justice to mercy. Consigning our enemies to God's justice and relishing the prospect that they are going to get what they deserve is one thing; it is quite another to ask God to show them mercy. Yet in some of his hardest teachings, Jesus pointed beyond the Psalms in just this way. "Love your enemies and pray for those who persecute you," he said (Matthew 5:44). "Forgive just as you are forgiven" (see Matthew 6:12, 14-15; 18:2-35). Over and over again he said it, and he demonstrated it in his dying words, "Father, forgive them; they do not know what they are doing" (Luke 23:34).

I prefer justice. I would rather be vindicated and see the tables turned on those who have hurt me. So it is hard to picture my enemies and then pray, "God, please bless John and Mary with all your blessings. Forgive them, and show them your mercy and kindness." That prayer tests my love, for it reveals whether forgiveness is still just words or whether it has taken root in my heart. I soon learn how far I have followed Jesus, who prayed specifically for my enemies and for me when he prayed, "Father, forgive them." To follow Jesus, I must prefer mercy.

How Much Longer?

The other prominent question in the lament songs is "How long?" "Yahweh, how long will you be?" (6:3). "How much longer will you forget me?" (13:1). "How much longer, Lord, will you look on?" (35:17). This agonizing question also belongs distinctly to people of faith, for it contains at least scraps of hope. "How much longer?" presumes that God must act to resolve the singer's distress. It rests on the conviction that God cannot and will not endlessly tolerate the menace of this moment. If the question whispers of hope, however, it cries out eloquently of anguish.

One of the principal reasons for the psalmists' distress is that, in the face of all their troubles, God seems to have abandoned them. The One who could rescue them seems to look on idly (35:17) or to be standing off to the side, having deserted them (38:21). The Almighty, on whom they have relied, seems to have forgotten about them at the worst possible time (13:1; 42:9; 44:24) and in shocking unconcern has even fallen asleep (44:23). These bold charges point to the crisis of our spirits—our sense of desperation and God's apparent distance. We need help *now*, not after God arises refreshed from an afternoon nap. We have trusted and prayed and pleaded, yet God seems to have left us to fend for ourselves, like nonswimmers thrown into deep waters. The water is up to our necks, and not even God will toss us a lifeline.

Sometimes God doesn't even seem to be standing by. The Presence of God has disappeared entirely. "How much longer will you hide your face from me" the singers implore (*see* 13:1; 44:24; 88:14). Could it be forever? Religious feeling fails completely, and the withering winds of God's hiddenness sear our souls, leaving a barren wasteland. Here we have entered the wilderness, the "night of the senses," the "dark night of the soul." In such times we long for the warmth, the inner assurances, the feelings that the God whom we love above all else is near. We even interrogate and accuse ourselves, ruthlessly searching for anything on our part that might block the intimacy that has slipped away from us. Yet we despair, like Job, that despite our eagerness and innocence, God seems nowhere to be found. Numbness and doubt overwhelm joy and confidence. "How long will you hide, Lord?" Perhaps worst of all is God's silence. "I call all day, my God, but you never answer," accuses one singer (22:2). Another pleads, "God whom I praise, break your silence" (109:1). Here is barrenness turned cold. Any response, even anger, would be better than no answer at all! In this lonely silence, experience shatters all easy platitudes about how God answers every prayer. Answers, indeed! In the silence we can almost hear our words of prayer tumble to the floor, and we may blush at how preposterous even attempting words seems. We wonder whether it really matters, whether we're even heard, let alone responded to, or whether prayer is merely a naive and comforting way of getting dreams and frustrations off our chests. As the hollow stillness seems filled only by our own words, sometimes we struggle to pray at all.

When we feel left on our own or are unable to feel or hear God, we may well join the ancient singers in pleading, "How much longer, Lord?" Though certainly it is a question tinged with hope, it is also a measure of our struggle as adventurers in faith.

How to Complain

The very fact that the lament songs abound in the Psalms suggests that they can teach us how to cope with struggle in the life of faith. The German Old Testament scholar Claus Westermann has observed that lament has been largely excluded from the Christian tradition,[3] and insofar as he is correct, it is a great loss. One of the best ways to meet our struggles is to learn from the psalmists how to complain.

The first lesson the Hebrew singers teach us is simply to be honest. Frankly, the honesty we need can easily elude us, particularly in the Christian subculture that prizes constant happiness and perpetual spiritual victory. In such settings (and even privately) it is much easier to smile and blithely praise God than to admit to spiritual struggles. If we are to progress in the inner life, however, we must acknowledge our despair, as well as our successes, to ourselves and to God.

"One of the best ways to meet our struggles is to learn from the psalmists how to complain."

Besides the psalmists, other Old Testament figures display the kind of integrity we need. Moses showed it, for example, when he was surrounded by sand, by the burdens of leadership, and by angry Israelites who had tried every manna recipe in the book. "Why do you treat your servant so badly?" he complained to God. "If this is how you want to deal with me, I would rather you killed me!" (Numbers 11:11, 15). To this we could add Elijah, Jeremiah, Job, and others who complained, argued, and

DESPAIRING

even accused God. Even if they didn't see their situations accurately, they were honest about their struggles. Perhaps their example can embolden the more timid of us, who have been taught the pragmatism of being polite, if false, to our betters. Lies born of courtesy and fear don't fool God and certainly don't help us. To deal with our struggle at all, we must at least be honest.

We must not, however, confuse being honest with merely being crabby. The lament songs make this clear as well, for they include much more than cries of distress and pleas for deliverance. One of the major elements in the lament is the singer's confession of trust in God. Another is some expression of assurance by the psalmist (or in words addressed to him) that his plea will be answered. A third typical element is praise, either lifted now or promised for the future. Thus the themes of trust, assurance, and praise move us sharply away from complaint alone.

To insist on the whole pattern of the lament is not just to protect God from constant whining, though such noise surely tests even the divine patience. Nor will proper complaint become an easy cure for our struggle. It can, however, push back despair by rekindling our hope.

Just as trust stands at the center of the lament song, sandwiched between moans of distress and cries for help, so it is central to the renewal of hope. The confession of trust, in this instance, works something like the magnifying glass I played with as a boy. I thought it a scientific marvel that by focusing the rays of the sun on a pile of dry, brittle leaves I could actually ignite a fire. In a similar way, declaring our trust gathers, like a glass, our scattered shreds of hope and intensifies them to kindle our spirits.

We must not, however, confuse confessions of trust with feelings of trust. When we are in despair, we may not feel trust at all. Indeed, our struggle is often over whether we even can trust. When we feel left in the lurch and ignored, feelings of trust do not come easily. In their stead, then, we must choose to trust. Trust becomes a matter of will.

Choosing to trust also requires that we remember. We must not seek to whip up feelings so much as to recall the character of God. Those who have known God can remember how God has helped them in the past. They can recount the traits of God's character, especially power, tenderness, and faithful love. By choosing to affirm what we have known of God, we focus those scattered recollections into a ray of hope.

I have often marveled at several people whom I consider to be modern "saints," particularly for the way that they can endure spiritual struggle. In their lives it seems that burden and serenity can walk hand in hand. The reason, I believe, is that they know God so well that they also know that any feelings of abandonment or betrayal can only be temporary and misleading, not final. "God will not forsake me," they insist. "God is not like that." Here is an important clue to meeting our questions "Why?" and our other struggles. Even when we are pushed to the wall of despair, we can choose to confess our trust. In our present distress, we, like the psalmists, can remember God's goodness. We can choose to answer the whys of doubt with "But God isn't like that."

To declare our trust also highlights the relationship already established between God and his people. The psalmists use it, to be sure, to try to prod God into action. But, more important, it establishes a context for our present distress. When we do not understand our circumstances or "what God is doing," we can still have confidence in that relationship. The point is not that God can deliver or has delivered, but that this God in whom we have trusted is our Deliverer. It is precisely such a binding relationship that Paul understands as he tells the Romans that nothing—persecution, attack, poverty, spiritual powers, even death itself—can separate us from the love of God. In fact, through these trials, "we triumph, by the power of him who loved us" (Romans 8:35-39). So the confessions of trust remind us, even in our wilderness, that we as people of God are sheltered and sustained by the One whose faithful love endures forever.

Pointing to this relationship not only connects us to the past, but also points with hope to the future. The psalmists vow to praise God for a future deliverance, and in making this promise, they anticipate that their relationship to God will continue. In the same way, when we can promise to praise, we declare, even in the face of trouble, that we have not been abandoned.

In teaching us how to complain, the lament songs suggest not only honesty and confession of trust, but also patience. The devotional masters often counsel patience during difficult times, but it may seem surprising to see it in the lamenting psalmists. After all, they often beg the Lord to "come quickly," and their urgent pleas frequently seem to border on hysteria. Surely we can understand how a singer who sees himself "on the brink of Sheol" might not say, "But take your time, Lord." Still, "come quickly" seems to shove patience aside.

In spite of that initial impression, patience and complaint can occur together, for complaint, at least in the Psalms, is rooted in hope. Complaint is not giving up. It grows, instead, out of believing that God will yet come to deliver. Job provides an ideal example of this point. For thousands of years now, Job has been lauded in story and maxim for his patience. Yet clearly he complained more bitterly than any other character in Scripture. The measure of his patience was not that he submitted quietly to his circumstances and to his self-righteous friends but that he refused to give up. Jesus told the story of a widow who badgered a judge until she finally got justice (Luke 18:1-8). Any parent knows how endlessly children can beg and whine as long as they think they still have a chance to get what they want. So there can be a confident patience in complaint, as there was for the psalmists, because it doesn't give up. It doesn't abandon hope.

Yet another dimension to patience is born of the knowledge that there are rhythms or cycles in the inner life. Certainly there will be times of ecstasy, when everything seems to go right and life is filled with joy. But barrenness, too, comes as a natural part of the rhythm of the spiritual life. Patience recognizes that such dryness may not symbolize failure, but may instead signal and stimulate continued growth.

Part of our struggle, of course, is to understand why such times come. Some writers suggest that God sends them to rouse us from spiritual sloth, to spur us on in our love for God, or to make us less dependent on our feelings and more dependent on God alone. Perhaps so. Because they have spurred my growth, I can imagine that God has sent me difficulties that have stripped away false securities and shattered hindering comforts. At the same time, some of our struggle clearly grows out of things that God has not sent to us, things that are evil and patently contrary to God's will. Yet in these, too, patience is required, for the process of God's victory over our circumstances and the healing of our spirits often takes time.

"Barrenness comes as a natural part of the rhythm of the spiritual life. Patience recognizes that such dryness may not symbolize failure, but may instead signal and stimulate continued growth."

Patience, then, recognizes and yields to the rhythms of the inner life. It both answers and is built into the psalmists' question, "How long?" Even to ask, "How much longer?" declares that the rhythm must change, that the dance will follow the dirge.

To learn from the psalmists' laments the ways of honesty, trust, and patience helps us when we are caught in despair. But even these, as useful as they are, supply neither easy formulae nor instant cures. There are none. Struggles will come. We'll be tempted to choose pious sham over truth. We may stammer our confessions of trust. Our cries for help may sound more pushy than patient. Yet for those who know God, that is not the whole story. The pulse of the Creator's heart resonates in the secret chambers of our own, so that we know somehow, deeply, that despair is not the last word. We know somehow that though we have had occasion to cry out, "God, why have you abandoned me?" we will yet say, "I will praise you before all peoples, for you have not hidden your face from me, and you have answered me when I called" (*see* 22:22-24).

F I V E

RESTING

Rest in God alone, my soul!
He is the source of my hope;
with him alone for my rock, my safety, my fortress,
I can never fall.

Psalm 62:5-6

While still a lad of seventeen, long before carving a niche for himself in the history of missions, Hudson Taylor shared with a minister in his hometown that God wanted him to go to China. Knowing that there were few missionaries in China at that time and that the way was very difficult, the minister asked Taylor how he proposed to go there. Taylor replied that he probably would need to follow the same pattern that Jesus had established for his disciples, going "without purse or scrip, relying on Him who had called me to supply all my need." Placing his hand on Taylor's shoulder, the minister tried to temper this youthful dream with the kindness of realism. "Ah, my boy," he advised, "as you grow older you will get wiser than that. Such an idea would do very well in the days when Christ Himself was on earth, but not now." In later years, after having founded the China Inland Mission, Taylor wrote, "I have grown older since then, but not wiser. I am more than ever convinced that if we were to take the direction of our Master and the assurances He gave to His first disciples more fully as our guide, we should find them to be just as suited to our times as to those in which they were originally given."[1]

Neither dreams nor patronizing smiles have disappeared in the century since Taylor's experience. I watch with hope and longing as I see my students stirred by the teaching and examples of trust of the Old Testament heroes, of Jesus and the Apostles, and of the daring pioneers of faith in the history of the church. Yet as they begin to share the dreams born in their hearts, I also cringe to see them smothered in the embrace of "older and wiser" arms that would hold them back from "resting in God alone." "It's wonderful to dream and to want to live with radical trust," we seem to say. "But that doesn't work in the real world. At some point you have to be practical."

If we are "wiser" by limiting the dimensions of trust, we are also sadder. We, too, would like to imitate those who trusted God with such grace, and we are drawn by biblical teachings that suggest trust in God alone is essential to know God at all. Yet because we "know better," because we live in a world where we have to pay the bills, please the boss, and play along with our culture, the saints seem touched with magic or madness, and the teachings of Scripture seem remote. Like the rich young ruler, we turn away in sadness. We wonder how, now that we are practical and wise, we can still trust God. That is the issue we must address in this chapter.

The psalmists urge trust in God, but we must see from the beginning that this trust is neither simple nor blind. I doubt very much that there is such a thing as "simple trust." For years

I have loved the stanza from John Greenleaf Whittier that begins, "In simple trust like theirs who heard, Beside the Syrian Sea,"[2] but trust seems less simple and innocent than that. Most of us have to learn what it means to trust God after our innocence has been stolen away and our naiveté has been shattered. The image of "childlike trust" appeals to us, of course, for we wish we could recover the freshness and naiveté of a child. However, our experience tells us that we can't trust so innocently and that our children mustn't either. "Don't talk to strangers," we tell our children who recognize no one as a stranger, because we know that children are sometimes kidnapped or abused. We know that, at least in some ways, the world is less charmed and wondrous than a child believes.

"Mature trust appears most clearly in the lives of those who have learned to rest in the midst of the storm."

Instead of "childlike trust," the reliance on God that can sustain us is a sturdy, knowing trust. It means resting in God in the face of despair, failure, the reality of evil, and not having easy answers to persistently perplexing questions. There is something akin to innocence in it, but it is innocence stripped of any Pollyanna notions about our world and our lives. That is why this chapter follows rather than precedes the chapter on despair. After having traveled through hiddenness and barrenness, seekers come into a mature, unshakable confidence in God's care and concern.

Mature trust appears most clearly in the lives of those who

have learned to rest in the midst of the storm. We see it in the cancer patient who remains at peace because she knows she is enveloped by God's love and power. We see it in those who endure persecution with serenity and joy. Often it is precisely those who have been stretched beyond their personal resources and who have faced life at its worst who have discovered best the truth of the psalmist's song, "In God alone there is rest for my soul" (62:1).

If trust is not simple, neither is it blind. It is not the sort of groundless belief once urged on me by a theology professor who, having failed to give an adequate rationale in support of one his favorite doctrines, advised me simply to accept it on faith. My youthful impertinence roused faculty suspicions for years to come, when I objected, "But you can believe virtually anything on that kind of baseless faith." Though my impertinence is now less youthful, the force of that objection still seems right. If faith is totally blind, then we can believe anything, whether truth or nonsense.

To those of the "God helps them that help themselves" school, whether believers or nonbelievers, the Bible may seem to be encouraging a foolish, blind trust. Unfortunately, some only confirm such skepticism by promoting a the-blinder-the-better approach to trust in God. But the Scriptures simply do not teach a faith without foundation. They call us not to a faith that is rational in the sense that it is grounded on logic, but to a faith that is perfectly reasonable because it has been proved over and over again in the laboratory of experience. As we shall see, the psalmists called us to a sturdy trust precisely because they knew from experience God's power, presence, and loyal love. They knew that, even when they could not anticipate exactly how God would care for them, God would be absolutely reliable. Blind trust was to them a completely foreign idea.

Maker of Heaven and Earth

One reason why the psalmists trust God is their vivid sense of God's creative power, which they see demonstrated in the founding and maintaining of the world. In one of the familiar Songs of Ascent, for example, the poet begins:

> *I lift my eyes to the mountains:*
> *where is help to come from?*
> *Help comes to me from Yahweh,*
> *who made heaven and earth.*

> —*Psalm 121:1-2*

To whom could we better turn for help? The psalmists tell us that we cannot find any greater security than relaxing into the powerful arms of the One who laid the earth's foundations, who determined the boundaries of the world, who controls the day and night and the seasons, and who "decides the number of the stars and gives each of them a name" (147:4; *compare* 74:16-17; 102:2-27; 146:5-6). We can trust the Maker of Heaven and Earth.

For the Hebrews, moreover, trusting God's power in creation went beyond simply an understanding of origins. The Almighty not only gave birth to the world of life and wonder that we enjoy, but also nurtures and sustains the creation millisecond by millisecond. "He provides for all living creatures," declares one singer (136:25), who is joined by another praising God for constantly renewing the world (104:27-30; *compare* 145:15-16). Because God's creative power is still active and not remote, we have reason to hope.

Hannah Whitall Smith shares the psalmists' vision of God at work, but presses it further to unmask our ambivalence about believing that such power can touch our own lives. "It is not hard, you find, to trust the management of the universe, and of all the outward creation, to the Lord. Can your case then be so much more complex and difficult than these, that you need to be anxious or troubled about his management of you?"³

These words encourage us, but they also point toward our difficulty in accepting them. Perhaps more than ever before, many of us find little relief in the idea that God's creative power can touch the troubles of our lives. Such a prospect seems too remote even to be possible. Even those who fiercely defend doctrines about creation often have a diminished sense of God as the Creator who fashioned and, more important, who still sustains the universe. Sometimes we act as if God stretched the seventh-day rest into a permanent vacation in the Heavenly Bahamas, leaving us to make do on our own. Often the doctrine of creation simply does not touch our lives deeply enough to increase our sense of trust.

> ## *"If we believe in a watchmaker God who wound up the world and who is now in forced retirement, it will be hard to imagine that the Creator's power can bear directly on our lives."*

Some of our ambivalence about our ability to trust God's power as Creator may rise from popular ideas about how the world works. Many still think, for example, that the world operates by a natural law so rigid that not even its Maker is welcome in it. Clearly, if we believe in a watchmaker God who wound up the world and who is now in forced retirement, it will be hard to imagine that the Creator's power can bear directly on our lives. We will be even less able to trust if we accept the popular idea that the origin and order of the world are basically random or accidental. It is a curious but real contradiction that many who would assent intellectually to a doctrine of creation still live as if rigid law and randomness govern their lives. Under the influence of such popular misconceptions, they experience God as remote and uninvolved.

The highly managed environments in which most of us live and our apparent mastery of the world may also diminish our sense of trust in a Creator God. Just as brightly lit streets dim our view of the Milky Way's sequined splendor, they may also obscure our vision of God. We can easily feel quite secure and self-sufficient in a culture in which street lights defeat the darkness, furnaces and air conditioners control the climate, and lavishly stocked supermarkets mask the ancient realities of seed, soil, and sunshine. The high level and rapid advance of technology can also beguile us into thinking that we can manage the world quite well without God's assistance. We can easily forget, in our daily rush, that it is still God "who covers the heavens with clouds, to provide the earth with rain, to produce fresh grass on the hillsides and the plants that are needed by man" (147:8).

As we underestimate the necessity of God's sustaining power, we also overestimate our own strength, overlooking, as God does not, the facts that "we are dust" (103:14) and our lives "only a puff of wind" (39:6, 11). The motto "In us we trust" is betrayed in our actions. As Thomas Kelly writes, "Too many of us rely upon God to do a few things for us, while we feel able to take care of the rest."[4] Our frequent failure to be grateful for even the simple things in our live—food, shelter, health, a paycheck—also discloses our pretension. The truth is that we are not left to our own resources. Whatever strength and resources we have, whether we recognize it or not, come from God.

I am not suggesting that we should sit idly by, waiting for God miraculously to fill our storage bins with grain or to make our outstanding balances disappear from the bank-card computers. The Old Testament wise men did, after all, commend the industry of the ant in harvesting (Proverbs 6:6-11). But we must learn to put our planning and hard work in the context of moment-by-moment confidence in God. When we get the promotion, win the bid, or bank our checks, we must not assume that our own energy, wisdom, and skill alone have brought the prosperity we have sought. Crops don't grow, businesses don't succeed, and careers don't blossom simply because we work hard. All these prosper because God is sustaining the earth and providing for our needs. God is continuing to give life.

One way we can increase our ability to trust is to recapture a sense of God's creative power. One positive step can be to cast out mistaken ideas that bedevil us in trying to understand God's relationship to the world. We can throw out, for example, the idea of a rigid natural law that excludes the Creator from the creation. We can abandon the idea that the world operates by mere randomness. It is neither scientifically necessary nor biblically accurate to say that our world is just a series of happy (or unhappy) accidents. We can also refuse to take sides in the bruising battle between creation theology and modern scientific theories. Though this issue still stirs great controversy, neither sound biblical teaching nor scientific theory in its proper limits requires such false and misleading choices. There is no sound reason that compels us to leave God out of our world.

Many more of us will grow in trust, however, by deepening our relationship with creation itself. Often we think clearly enough, but we experience too little. We fail to rest in God's creative power because we don't see it at work. Though "the heavens declare the glory of God" (19:1), the noise of our lives deafens us to their voice. If we would, we could recapture confidence in the Creator by giving up the dash of our Mad Hatter lives and opening ourselves instead to wonder. It isn't far from any of us. Even in cities birds nest and squirrels bounce across the lawn and balance precariously in giant maple trees. We can see the wonder of life as our children grow or as we tend the plants in our homes and gardens. We can learn about and revel in the intricacies and the immensity of the creation. Even better, we can go to wild, unspoiled places that can astonish us, that can teach us of life that is given, not managed, and that can sing to us songs of trust about the One in whose arms all life, even now, is embraced.

Marvels Among Us

A refrain often bears the message the songwriter doesn't want you to forget. So when one psalmist kept repeating, "Let these thank Yahweh for his love, for his marvels on behalf of men" (107:8, 15, 21, 31), he wanted to make sure his hearers rejoiced to know that, as another said, the "author of saving acts throughout the earth" (74:12) was among them. The Hebrews could trust God because they were convinced that the powerful Creator was present in their ordinary existence. They could rely on God being near rather than far away, in the midst of their lives instead of at the edge of the universe.

As witness to God's nearness, the Old Testament singers rehearsed a litany of deliverance, beginning with their dramatic rescue from the oppression of Pharaoh and reaching to their own times. "In you our fathers put their trust," they sang. "They trusted and you rescued them; . . . they never trusted you in vain" (22:4-5). In a thanksgiving song, another recalls, "I was pressed, pressed, about to fall, but Yahweh came to my help; Yahweh is my strength and my song, he has been my saviour" (118:13-14). Even the times in which they saw God judging them revealed the Divine Presence in their common lives. The theme of God's nearness floods the Psalms and all of the Old Testament, and it grows to become the central theme of the New Testament when in Jesus the reality of *Immanuel,* "God with us," takes its most radical turn.

"God's Presence is steadier and subtler than we generally imagine. Sometimes God may sign the sky in a spacious scrawl or etch fine characters on a palace wall, but mostly the name above all names is penciled lightly."

Even though it is central to the whole biblical story, we still struggle with the idea of God's nearness. We shut God out of history as easily as out of creation, particularly in times of despair. There are days, certainly, when the events of the world and of our lives are so uniformly dark that we can scarcely imagine that God is within a million light-years of our little planet, let alone in the midst of our common life. But even in less troubled times, we are prone to doubt.

Sometimes we fail to see God's Presence because we mistakenly imagine that it will always be dramatic or highly visible. We tend to think that the ordinary events of our lives result from "natural" causes, so we attribute to God only those things that we can't explain any other way. When doctors and drugs effect a cure, for example, we too easily credit only medical science and normal healing processes. For many of us, it is only when a cure comes after the doctors admit being baffled and declare the case hopeless that we recognize the hand of God. This way of thinking, however, is quite impractical. On the one hand, it casts us out of the arena of God's care by suggesting that most of the time we're on our own. On the other hand, it reduces God to a comic-book hero who rushes in at the last desperate moment of crisis to rescue us when "natural" means fail. God becomes Superman in a phone booth or the Cosmic White-Hat Cowboy, untying fair maidens from railroad tracks.

God's Presence is steadier and subtler than we generally imagine. Sometimes God may sign the sky in a spacious scrawl or etch fine characters on a palace wall, but mostly the name above all names is penciled lightly on walls, alongside "Kilroy was here" and "For a good time call. . . ." If we can train our eyes to read graffiti as well as billboards, we can begin to see the movements of grace in what appears ordinary. In due time we will see that "God with us" is the normal, natural state of affairs and that, because of this, our trust is not misplaced.

One way to learn to see God's nearness as normal is to hear deeply the stories and witness of others. The stories of biblical heroes help us at this point, and that is one reason why many of the Psalms recount God's work in Israel's history. Yet because people like Sarah, Moses, and David often seem remote and bigger than life, we sometimes must learn from other stories as well. Reading the biographies and autobiographies of people of faith like Hudson Taylor, Francis of Assisi, George Mueller, and Agnes Sanford opens our eyes to the reality of God near us and the possibilities that creates for our living. However, since even lives such as these sometimes seem just out of reach, we do well to listen also to the stories of God at work that we tell each other. Daniel, the ancient wise man; Augustine, the saintly bishop; Joe, the gas-station operator; and Marti, the school-teacher, all can remind us that God is with us.

Perhaps an even better way to develop a keener eye is to learn to see God at work in our own lives. In keeping a spiritual journal, for example, one could incorporate a regular section for a "God Hunt," a term suggested by David and Karen Mains of the Chapel of the Air.[5] The God Hunt is simply reflecting on the events of the day and recording the places where we can see signs of God's Presence. Obvious answers to prayer, unexpected evidences of God's care, uncanny "coincidences," and awareness of help in doing God's work in the world all qualify as bona fide sightings. As simple as it is, this is a profoundly helpful practice. By gradually revealing the patterns of God's faithfulness, it can rescue us from the trap of immediacy and from the blinding preoccupation we have with the problems which confront us in this moment. Even better, it trains us to recognize more readily and more often that God is indeed among us.

Learning to see God's work day-to-day also helps us to trust even when the power of evil obscures our view. Times come, inevitably, when our trust in God seems wasted and promises like "no disaster can overtake you" (91:10) seem hollow. Yet when disaster does come, we need not dismiss the language of trust as mere poetic exaggeration. If there is hyperbole, there is also the profound truth of experience that God is indeed among us. We know that God's will is not always done, and we puzzle over some of the things that happen to us, but even then we need not imagine that God is absent or has been vanquished. The "Shelter" of our lives has not been toppled. Joseph's remark to his brothers, who had years earlier sold him into slavery, points to God's nearness even in disaster. "The evil you planned to do to me," he said, "has by God's design been turned to good" (Genesis 50:20). Trusting God neither inoculates us against life nor insures that we will always understand what happens, but it does guarantee that the One who watches over us day and night will always be near. Because in gloomy times as well as in glad we cannot escape God's Presence, there is reason to "rest in God alone."

Pursuing Love

To know both God's power and God's Presence in the world does not in itself provide an adequate basis for trust. In fact, such convictions can easily bring fear, instead of hope, if we are not also convinced of God's love. A powerful god who is also malicious or capricious can threaten rather than reassure. We know, of course, that this is not just a theoretical problem. In many religions, ancient and modern, the specter of an angry god has brought fear and cowering obedience. Even in contemporary Christianity, despite its emphasis on divine love, great numbers of believers see God more as an angry Judge than as a loving Friend. To be persuaded of anger rather than love brings restlessness instead of rest.

The ancient Hebrews struggled, just as we do, to strike the balance between God's anger and love. Readers who have only a casual acquaintance with the Old Testament often fail to appreciate this point, convinced by glimpses of judgment speeches and stormy images that the Hebrew God was merely angry and capricious. This is not the view, however, that the Hebrews themselves held. For them, even wrath and judgment were encompassed by love. "Righteous in all that he does, Yahweh acts only out of love" (145:17), they sang, declaring that, on balance, love prevailed over all.

The word the Hebrews used to talk of God's love is so sturdy and rich that we don't even have a single English word adequate to translate it. For this wonderful word, *hesed,* translators have used, among others, "love," "kindness," "steadfast love," "lovingkindness," and "grace." Yet none of these words fully conveys the Hebrews' sense of God's love. This love does not waver and is always loyal. It is about this love that the poet of the Shepherd Psalm sings when he writes, "Ah, how goodness and *hesed* pursue me, every day of my life" (23:6). *Hesed* is both strong and tender, a love that reaches as high as the heavens (36:5; 57:10; 103:11). This is the remarkable love which the Old Testament so frequently praises as "everlasting" (136:1-26).

It is not surprising, then, that the psalmists often point to such reliable love as a reason to trust. "Grace *[hesed]* enfolds the man who trusts in Yahweh" (32:10) they declared, urging their hearers to "see how the eye of Yahweh is . . . on those who rely on his love *[hesed]*" (33:18). They even connect this conviction with the fortress language that is so common to the theme of trust in the Psalms: "My citadel is God himself, the God who loves *[hesed]* me" (59:17). It is the power of this kind of love that overcomes fear (1 John 4:18) and leads us to rest in God.

How much further ahead we would be if we could see that God pursues us with love! Being neither hostile nor apathetic, God actively envelops our lives with tender care. It is precisely this active concern that Jesus emphasized when he told his disciples not to worry about tomorrow. Today, he said, has enough troubles of its own, but even these will be cared for by the One who clothes the lilies in exquisite garments and provides for the birds daily all that they need. Jesus presses the point even further by insisting that those who worry instead of trusting God's loving care are acting like pagans, rather than like people of faith (Matthew 6:2-34).

Oil and Water

God's power, Presence, and love, then, come together to establish a solid foundation on which to build trust. Translated into practice, to trust means to be convinced that God is fully aware of our circumstances, is present in the midst of them, and is acting in wisdom, power, and love to accomplish what is best for us. I suspect that, as often as not, this conviction will be one we must consciously choose rather than naturally feel. And it does become for us, in a sense, a black-and-white choice. As Hannah Whitall Smith writes: "Remember always that there are two things which are more utterly incompatible even than oil and water, and these two are trust and worry."[6]

Worry clearly signals that we have not yet fully learned how to rest in God alone. Playing out in our minds "worst scenarios," mentally and physically triple-checking on tasks or people, hedging the bet of faith with backup systems—all these reveal how far we have yet to go in trust. In replying to worriers seeking to excuse themselves by pleading, "I don't have enough faith," Hannah Smith narrows the issue to its central point. What you mean, she says, is that you don't have faith in God.[7]

On a recent winter day, my wife, Margi, was caught in traffic on a dangerously icy bridge. Part of her natural response was to pray for God's protection, but as she started across the bridge she noticed that her knuckles were white from gripping the steering wheel and her heart was in her throat. She was brought up short by the thought, *If I'm trusting God to answer my prayer, then why is my heart pounding?* Even when we allow for natural surges of adrenaline, pounding hearts often betray the real character of our trust.

"At times the need to retain control springs out of wanting God to be our lackey instead of our Lord."

We are also betrayed when, by insisting on being in control, we cannot release our problems to God. Sometimes this may rise out of a misguided sense of self-reliance that suggests that relying on anyone else, including God, is a sign of weakness. At other times the need to retain control springs out of wanting God to be our lackey instead of our Lord. Both personally and corporately, we too easily make plans and carry them out, only then remembering to invite God to prosper them. Such behavior shuts God out, denying the Divine Presence among us. Instead of attaching God to our plans like a device to supercharge them, trust requires that all our decision making, planning, and action go forward in the context of God's life around us and within us. Trust requires that we submit as fully to guidance as to protection and provision. A quick formal prayer before we rush on to do things our own way entirely misses the point. How badly we need to control and manipulate the events of our lives can also serve as a measure of how fully we trust God.

We can increase our ability to trust by submitting ourselves to questions about where our trust does, in fact, lie. For example, how directly is my peace of mind conditioned by my bank account? What things in my life really make me feel secure? How long has it been since I have taken any genuine risks for God? What pulls me back from risk? In what measure must I be able to create a safety net of my own? How much visible evidence do I need to believe that God is with me? What things may seriously rival God for my trust? Questions of this sort, honestly considered, can both reveal our points of weakness and suggest ways to overcome them.

We can also increase trust by, like weight lifters and runners in training, pushing to the limits of our strength. Under God's guidance, we can stretch our comfort zones and choose to take some risks. Those who too easily rely on money probably need to give more of it away. Many have witnessed to spiritual growth that has come through giving generously, even when it seemed impossible. Those who gain security through power and manipulation, whether it's running the office or bossing the kids, need to exercise power less and become more vulnerable. Those who are overly secure in the good opinion of others might risk that reputation in loving service to God. Some, surely, should leave the carpeted living rooms of the Bible studies for the tile-floored soup kitchens of the slums. What is required will be different, of course, for each one, but whatever has become idolatrous, whatever we rely on instead of on God, must be broken.

"Rest in God alone" is more than pleasant religious prattle. It is both practical and realistic. Because the God of all life is with us in power and in love, we can rest easy, knowing that, in comparison to the Eternal One, every other hope for security is deceptive and transitory. As we examine and discipline ourselves, consciously choosing to rely only on God, we shall come more and more readily to confess to our Maker, "My refuge, my fortress, my God in whom I trust" (91:2).

SIX

CONVERSING

Lord, in trouble I invoke you,
and you answer my prayer.

Psalm 86:7

P rayer doesn't really accomplish anything," the minister's wife counseled confidently. "It is simply a way of getting things off your chest." For Melanie, who was already struggling to have faith at all, this declaration jolted her so hard that, as far as I know, she has never recovered. And for good reason. If getting things off our chests is, indeed, all there is to prayer, then we would do just as well to visit a psychiatrist, work out our frustrations on the racquetball court, or unload our troubles on a sympathetic friend—all practices commonly taken up instead of prayer. Why keep up the pretense of prayer, if God is uninterested? Only if God listens and responds does prayer make any sense at all.

I was startled, too, but in quite a different way, one time when a friend of mine began to pray. As the two of us strolled along the beach, bantering and debating, I hardly expected her to invite anyone else into the conversation. "Jesus," she began abruptly, and as we walked along she went on to ask for guidance about the problem that had been puzzling us. Already I believed that God is near us and desires to be involved in our daily lives. But she acted as if it were true, as if "God with us" had been with us all along.

In the years since that day at the beach I have grown to enjoy bringing God into the give-and-take of a discussion, to visiting with this Friend while driving, or to sharing jokes and yearnings with him over dinner at a restaurant. Such an informal, anywhere, eyes-open style of praying sometimes surprises others as much as it did me, particularly those who know only heads-bowed, eyes-closed prayers, laced liberally with *thees* and *thous*. If it surprises us, however, it also points toward an understanding of prayer that many of us sorely need.

The contrast between these two stories highlights the ambivalence and confusion about prayer that we often experience. Beyond being a commendable religious duty, where does prayer fit into ordinary living? Does it make any genuine difference? How can I learn to pray so that it seems life-giving and important? Such common questions can both puzzle and hinder us, but here again the Psalms can help, by pointing to prayer that rises above mere formal phrases or routine patter, to expectant dialogue with the God who hears.

The way in which the Psalms teach us about prayer is somewhat different from what we have seen in other chapters of this book. Certainly prayer is a distinct impulse or movement of the heart, but it is also a vehicle for our other responses to God. Through prayer we often express our longing, our repentance, our despair, or our praise. Because the Psalms are, indeed, the prayer book of the Bible, they more often teach us what prayer is like through example than through direct instruction. They illustrate the elements of dialogue with God, for instance, but don't talk about it extensively. Nonetheless, these songs of prayer, supported by other biblical teaching, reveal a liberating approach to conversing with God, one we would do well to comprehend and practice.

The Dialogue

Trusting and praying both grow out of the same root. If we are to do either, we must assume that God is present in power and love, because when we lack these convictions, prayer turns into dusty verbiage. At the practical level, this poses a greater problem for those who do pray than for those who never bother. Many of the students with whom I work, for example, pray for guidance about major life decision—their vocations, courses of study, marriage—yet their actions often betray their doubt that God will actually teach them what they need to do. I myself flounder at times in trying to pray for leaders of church and government, because too often it seems difficult to imagine God actively influencing their work. Others around me are timid to pray for healing, either because they believe implicitly that this is beyond what God is willing or able to do or that, to put it in its best light, in these days God has entrusted all such matters to doctors and natural law. In all these instances, prayer becomes weak and flabby, for only when we are grounded in a sturdy trust in God's loving, powerful Presence can we build the life of prayer.

Beyond this essential foundation, the Bible portrays prayer as a dialogue. It intends to teach something far more significant, of course, than that prayer as conversation is idly chatting with the Almighty. Instead, through stories about individuals at prayer and through a great variety of Psalms, the Bible shows that God speaks to us and hears us and that we can hear and speak to God. "Prayer at its highest," writes Frank Laubach, "is a two-way conversation."[1] God desires to converse personally with everyone.

Many people, feeling unworthy, inadequate, or insignificant, can hardly imagine that this might be true. "Why should God listen to someone like me?" they ask. "Maybe God listens to some people—saintly grayheads, preachers, and the like but, Lord knows, I'm not one of those. I'm not good enough to pray; I don't know how to pray; and when I try, it seems as if the words just bounce around inside and nothing happens." So in frustration and weakness, many rely on the prayers of pastors and godly friends or do not pray at all. In discouragement and disbelief, they miss the dialogue of prayer.

It can help us a great deal to remember how prominent the personal dimension of prayer is in Scripture. The Bible often recounts divine-human conversations, some initiated by God and others initiated by man, and many of them have a more vigorous tone than we commonly associate with prayer. Abraham bargains with God over the fate of Sodom. Moses and Amos both plead with God to show mercy, while Jonah complains that he would just as soon die, because God is too merciful. As Hannah prays, she pours out her heart so intensely that the priest Eli thinks she is drunk, yet through him she receives God's reply that she will have the son she has so earnestly requested. Perhaps more than any other, the example of Jesus seeking the will of the Father reminds us that we should expect prayer to be conversational.

Even the forms of prayer in the Bible are inherently personal. Old Testament scholar Moshe Greenberg, in his fine work *Biblical Prose Prayer,* shows, for example, that the very patterns of prayer in the Old Testament are based on natural, human patterns of speech.[2] Though the Psalms are more stylized and liturgical, they, too, reveal that dialogue in prayer is exactly what we should expect. Not only do the psalmists frequently testify, "I called, and he answered," but we also see some of the answers. In a number of the Psalms, for example, we see words of assurance from God, perhaps given through the priest, in response to the singer's prayer. Because the entire body of biblical teaching is so clear, it does not surprise us to think that, like Moses, we can talk with God as a person would talk with a friend (Exodus 33:11).

~

"Biblical prayer is personal, not magical; dialogue, not demand."

Talking to God personally differs entirely from trying to put the Almighty under our thumbs with prayers born of magic and ritual. Yet many people, ancient and modern, have treated prayer more as incantation than dialogue. Many of ancient Israel's neighbors, certainly, tried to sway the will of the gods by spreading sumptuous banquets for them in their temples and by flawlessly reciting prescribed prayers. Israel herself fell into this trap at times, but was sharply rebuked for presuming that God is more interested in formal phrases, fasts, and festivals than in loyal love toward God and neighbor (*see* Psalm 50 and throughout the prophets). Israel, at her best, knew that prayer is not manipulation and hocus-pocus.

Modern Christians, at their best, know that, too, but practices of prayer akin to magic persist widely in the Christian movement. For example, some pray as if they will be heard the better for their flowery language or impassioned style.

Others insist that certain postures, patterns, and phrases must be used if prayer is to be effective. Still others presume on grace, thinking that by "laying claim" to "promises" they find in Scripture, they put God under obligation to do as they ask. In such sub-Christian and unbiblical expressions of prayer, what once may have been vital has degenerated into idle form. Biblical prayer is personal, not magical; dialogue, not demand.

Listening and Answering

Prayer has less to do with getting things than with knowing God. It is more concerned with loving God than with lists of prayer requests. Asking for assistance and knowing God are related, of course, but coming into intimacy with the Holy One is the principal purpose and context of prayer. We want to be molded to the life and will of our Eternal Friend. We see this clearly in the life of Brother Giles, who was regarded by his Franciscan brothers as a master of prayer and was so close to God that he felt he was "plundering joy." Giles said, "He who does not know how to pray does not know God."[3] Jesus saw the same connection between being granted what we ask in prayer and intimacy when he told his disciples that as long as they remained in him, just as branches are connected to the vine, they could ask what they would and get it (John 15:1-7).

To pray primarily in order to know God moves us toward the root of what it means for prayer to be personal, and it can change our attitude toward praying. I recently read a magazine article in which the writer protested that the current emphasis on spiritual discipline is a return to legalism. In particular, he spurned the need to pray regularly, likening our relationship with God to that we have with close friends with whom we may converse easily, even if we have not talked with them for a long time. I, like most of us, have friends like that, of course, but there is not a single one whom I would deliberately ignore for long periods of time. On the contrary, these are the friends I am eager to be with as often as I can. So it is with God. Rather than feeling legalistically that we "ought" to be praying, we can want increasingly to pray because of the ever-deepening connectedness we have with this Eternal Friend. The great French master of prayer, Jean-Nicholas Grou, described this when he wrote, "Love God and you will be always speaking to him. Ask God to open your heart and kindle in it a spark of his love; then you will begin to understand what praying means."[4] Indeed, as our longing for God expressed through prayer draws us into an intimate knowledge of the holy, we discover that in a profound sense "God himself is the answer to prayer."[5]

Out of this kind of intimacy the dialogue of prayer blossoms—the listening and answering, the speaking and being heard. Listening, of course, should be our first responsibility in this conversation, though I suspect that in the practice of prayer many of us are among those whom Clement described as being "like old shoes—all worn out but the tongue."[6] Because of our incessant chatter, our failure to wait in stillness, we too easily drown out what God is trying to say to us. We would do far better to join with the psalmists as they often request divine teaching (25:4-5; 27:11; 119), knowing that God has responded with the promise: "I will instruct you, and teach you the way to go; I will watch over you and be your adviser" (32:8).

One of the things God wants to teach us directly, if we would listen, is how to pray. The One who hears our prayers is also the One who desires to lead us beyond our weakness in trying to pray as we should. The key is listening. In recalling Pentecost and how the first disciples waited in prayer for the Holy Spirit, William Penn points out, "If so much waiting and preparation by the Spirit was required to fit them to preach to man, some waiting at least may be needed to fit us to speak to God."[7] Penn's point is critical to effective prayer. I fear that we often fail to wait, but instead pray hastily and thoughtlessly, using trite sentiments and phrases. We promise too quickly and too flippantly to pray for certain situations or to pray in certain ways. If we really want God's will to be done, we must be patient to learn what it is. It may not require a long period of searching, but it will demand at least an attitude of listening and obedience. God will teach those who wait attentively not only the general ways of prayer, but also very specifically how to pray.

This moves us well beyond such easily contrived blanket prayers as, "Bless this mess," or, "Please help Patty and John." Instead, as we wait for divine guidance, we can learn what matters we should take up in prayer and how we should pray for them. This is obviously not the province of rote or written prayers, but I have frequently seen such guidance in my experience. I have often heard the subjects of prayer exclaim to those who have prayed for them, "How did you know?" or, "That was exactly right!" because God had guided those attentive in prayer to use the words or images most needed in that situation. Such guidance may come in many ways—impressions, nudges, images, inner words, Scripture, the increase of compassion for particular concerns. Often it helps to ask questions in prayer to understand better how to approach a particular problem. If we will listen, God will indeed teach us specifically how to pray. In fact, we can be so thoroughly submitted to God's guidance that we may experience almost as an observer that "prayer is taking place" or that we are being "prayed through."[8]

Given the fact that God will guide our prayers, it is surprising how often people suggest that such a dialogue is no longer possible. Because they are told that God, who once spoke with individuals person-to-person, now usually responds to us only through an inspired book, many people do not even expect to be in conversation with God, and not anticipating it, they miss this great privilege of dialogue almost altogether. Any such loss is both tragic and unnecessary. Part of the point of the Bible, after all, is to show us how God communicates with people. Even to hint that, over the centuries, God has drawn back and become reluctant to guide or answer those who pray teaches an idea that contradicts the Scriptures, the witness of the faithful, and common sense. God desires to converse with us as freely as ever.

In addition to listening, genuine prayer is answering what we have heard. "The great Christian men and women of prayer," writes Douglas Steere, "have always looked upon prayer as a *response* to the ceaseless outpouring love and concern with which God lays siege to every soul."[9] Biblical prayer suggests that this answering might take several forms— assent or complaint, pleading or puzzlement, thanksgiving or praise. Our final answer in prayer, however, is to say yes to God's purposes.

Such a yes is part of the personal risk of prayer, for if we are to pray seriously, we must answer by submitting our own lives to transformation. "To pray is to open oneself to the possibility of sainthood," writes Kenneth Leech, "to the possibility of becoming set on fire by the Spirit."[10] It is the kind of risk in prayer that the psalmist took in saying, "God, examine me and know my heart, probe me and know my thoughts" (139:23). One does not pray such words lightly, as I discovered anew recently while praying that a quarreling group to which I belong would begin to get along again. The prayer doubled back on me when God showed me that before I could continue to pray for others to be reconciled, I must first forgive, abandon my own anger, and be willing to do my part to repair those relationships. To answer in prayer often means to permit God to refine and recreate us first.

"Clearly God has chosen that we should help get holy work done in the world, and one of the principal ways of working together with God is prayer."

To say yes (or amen) to God's guidance in prayer is also to answer, "Thy will be done," a phrase much sturdier and more joyous than we commonly think. To desire God's will, in the biblical way of thinking, is to long for the best world possible. The Torah Psalms, for example, lavish praise on the life-giving wonder of God's decisions and decrees (19:7-14; 119), while in other Psalms all creation joyously anticipates seeing the rule of God completely established (96; 98). With his disciples, Jesus perpetuated this same desire by teaching them to pray, "Thy kingdom come. Thy will be done on earth as it is in heaven." Realistically, if God is both loving and wise, how could we reasonably want anything else? How could we, even out of self-interest, fail to answer, "Thy will be done"?

Answering by truly praying, "Thy will be done," also helps make it so. Though I do not fully understand the reasons why, it simply happens that when we join our will to God's in prayer, we help release the Almighty's power in the world. I know well that at times such an idea seems preposterous, but it is true.

Clearly God has chosen that we should help get holy work done in the world, and one of the principal ways of working together with God is prayer. Through our prayers or lack of them, we can help or hinder God's purposes. So a very practical part of the answering of prayer is, after learning what God is doing or wants to do, to pray specifically that it will be so.

To say, "Thy will be done," in this way is quite different from what we commonly hear in practice. This is a sturdy prayer, not a prayer of timid resignation. Yet often it seems that people use this powerful phrase to mask the hesitancy of their prayers. Some frankly don't know God's will from their own, either thinking that God's will is wholly inscrutable or never having learned to listen to God's teaching. I have seen others lift impassioned petitions to the Lord, only to mumble in a hangdog tone at the end, "Thy will be done," obviously expecting that nothing will come of their prayers. Often God is generous with us even in such weakness, but there is a better way. We can learn God's ways so that we can pray with joy and confidence, "Yes! Thy will be done!"

Simple and Sincere

In emphasizing the importance of listening in prayer, I am not suggesting that, as employees of minor rank and children are sometimes told, we should "speak only when spoken to." The psalmists' common refrain, "I cried, he answered," shows quite clearly that we don't need a royal summons to pray. We can learn ways to speak with God without sounding like telephone solicitors who apparently never need to breathe. The dialogue of prayer can become a natural, steady part of our lives.

Over the years, however, I have noticed that prayer does not seem natural for a lot of people. Rhonda, for example, simply could not pray aloud with others, though she wanted to, mainly because she feared she couldn't handle the complexities of prayer language without embarrassing herself. To use the proper forms and tenses of all the *thees* and *thous* and *dosts* and *doests* as well as sustain reverential inflections and strategically insert grand epithets for God all at the same time were simply overwhelming. Prayer was too distant and difficult.

> ## *"Do not think to overcome the Almighty by the best material put in the aptest phrase. No. One groan, one sigh from a wounded soul, excels and prevails with God."*
> ### —William Penn

One way of overcoming such difficulties is to learn from the prayers of others. The Psalms have guided learners in prayer for millennia now, and for good reason. After all, how could one improve on "May the words of my mouth always find favour, and the whispering of my heart, in your presence, Yahweh" (19:14) or "Create in me a clean heart, O God" (51:10, KJV)? A friend of mine once told me she learned to pray by repeatedly using John Baillie's *A Diary of Private Prayer.* And how many millions have been helped by *The Book of Common Prayer?* I myself, who once thought written prayers were wicked and who smirked, in my youth, at clergy who couldn't pray without a script, rushed to buy *The Book of Common Prayer* just to have the grand words of praise that begin, "Therefore with Angels and Archangels, and with all the company of heaven, we laud and magnify thy glorious Name."[11] To these prayers we could add those of Lancelot Andrewes, Sören Kierkegaard, Michel Quoist, and many others. As we soak in their phrases and cadences, all of them can help us learn the ways of prayer.

These classic prayers, if we misuse them, can also hinder us, for we may come to think that to pray well—or at all—we must mimic their lofty sentiments and wonderful words. Though we may well learn from them helpful language for prayer, nothing could be further from the truth. As William Penn counsels, "Do not think to overcome the Almighty by the best material put in the aptest phrase. No. One groan, one sigh from a wounded soul, excels and prevails with God."[12] The sublimest prayers of all must not blind us to the fact that real prayer is simple.

God delights in simple prayers from ordinary people. Though many of the Psalms seem quite sophisticated and liturgical, many others and the rest of the prayers of the Old Testament demonstrate this simplicity. Clearly anyone could pray and be heard, from Moses to Samson to the pagan sailors who fed Jonah to the savage waves. Moreover, the patterns of prayers were simple, like the dialogue one would have with other people in everyday life.[13] Jesus made essentially the same point when he taught his disciples the simple Lord's Prayer, warning them not to babble on like pagans who think they will be heard for the abundance of their words (Matthew 6:7-13). As far as the Bible is concerned, you don't have to be a star or an orator in order to pray.

To pray conversationally can help us keep it simple. Although I have written of praying informally on the beach, in the car, or at the restaurant, the point is not that prayer should be casual, though it often liberates people to discover that they need not be bound by prescribed postures, places, and phrases. What we need is prayer that is real and that flows out of our own lives with authentic words of longing, despair, trust, and praise. Simple, conversational prayer helps bring to life the reality that God is near and not remote.

Effective prayer must also be sincere, for the efficacy of prayer has much more to do with one's relationship to God than with proper technique. The Psalms sharply contrast those who in prayer "outwardly flattered him, and used their tongues to lie to him" (78:36) with those "who call upon him in truth" (145:18, RSV) or "with sincerity." To pray sincerely means to be honest and vulnerable before God, opening ourselves wholeheartedly to this Friend. To put it in the vernacular, it is spilling our guts to God. This is what Thomas Kelly describes when he writes, "Back behind the scenes of daily occupation you offer yourself steadily to God, you pour out all your life and will and love before Him, and try to keep nothing back. Pour out your triumphs before Him. But pour out also the rags and tatters of your mistakes before Him."[14] In the sincerity of keeping nothing back we can learn to share with God even the most ordinary matters. I have often hesitated at this point, perhaps being reluctant to be embarrassed again over my failures or not wanting to trouble the Almighty with small things. God, of course, does not despise the small. After all, Jesus taught us, the Creator knows even the number of hairs on our heads (Matthew 10:30). When we are unable to pray easily about the small things, I suspect it is because we have not yet fully understood how far-reaching God's love really is. We cannot quite imagine an intimate love that encompasses even the details of our lives. As I have learned more of God's love, it has become easier to tell God of my concerns over my daily schedule, the family budget, or the way I father my children. Despite some progress, however, my friends still have occasion to laugh at me over my reluctance to pray for parking places and other minutiae of daily life. Yet I am learning ever more clearly that part of sincere conversation with God is small talk.

Constant and Confident

Such a life of simple, sincere prayer leads naturally to the dialogue of prayer as a steady habit. Praying, we discover, does not need to be limited at all, but can become very nearly a running conversation fully integrated into the cycle of our living. The psalmists point in this direction when they sing of meditating on God's Law continually or praising God's Name without ceasing. So do the saints when they speak of continual prayer and practicing the Presence of God. Certainly we ought not abandon prayer in set times and places, but to talk with God only in such times leaves us far short of what is possible. Is there any activity which we cannot consciously share with this Companion? Is there any place that is off-limits or inaccessible to this Friend? There is nothing, really, to prevent us from praying, silently or aloud, as circumstances may require, behind the desk or at the counter, on the court or by the pool. To converse with God only on our knees or in the sanctuary is consciously or by default, at least, to leave God out of the greater part of our lives.

Continual prayer eventually moves us even beyond words. "To pray . . . means to think and live in the presence of God," writes Henri Nouwen. "The main question, therefore, is not so much what we think, but to whom we present our thoughts."[15] Every word, every action, and every thought can be gathered into this holy conversation so that at last our whole lives are prayer and we are firmly anchored each moment in the Eternal.

"To converse with God only on our knees or in the sanctuary is consciously or by default, at least, to leave God out of the greater part of our lives."

Experiencing prayer as a dialogue also gives us greater freedom to experiment with prayer. Frankly, the best way to learn how to pray is by using the experimental method. This is basically what a dear woman, who is unusually effective in prayer, told me several years ago when I asked her to teach me how to pray. "Just pray," she said patiently, and virtually all the giants of prayer would agree with her. Learn by doing, and don't be afraid of not getting it "right." Probably this experimental attitude is what has made the writings of Agnes Sanford and Frank Laubach so helpful for so many. "Pray *whenever you think of it,"* urges Laubach.[16] Pray for the people you encounter in everyday life. Quietly scatter blessings on strangers in the airline terminal or at the grocery store. Pray for the people who come to mind and for the events and people you hear of in the news.[17] In her writings, Agnes Sanford often counsels us to start with small, tangible subjects for prayer and to allow God to use our imaginations as a means of teaching us how to pray and of increasing our faith.[18] Through the laboratory of experience, we can learn to pray for the common cold and for cancer, for wisdom and for peace, and even for the creation, from roses and geraniums to the San Andreas Fault! As we experiment with prayer, we can even ask God what we're missing or how we should pray differently to have greater effect. Experiment as you converse with God, and through this, learn how to pray.

The experiment has almost no bounds about either how you pray or for what you pray. In addition to private prayer, it helps us to pray in groups. I have discovered new insights by meeting regularly with one of my friends to pray and to explore new prayer territory. Try praying with the laying on of hands, a practice prominently mentioned in the New Testament and one that still helps transmit God's power. On the assumption that God doesn't have to pay extra charges to be in on the conversation, some of the most meaningful times of prayer I have experienced have been over the telephone. None of these are stunning innovations, I am sure, but they suggest that there are many ways in which we can pray. We can also experiment in praying about many different things. In my little circle, we have prayed for mending broken collarbones to healing broken relationships and for overcoming fear and anger to cutting off destructive channels of spiritual influence. To this we could add prayer for jobs, the buying and selling of houses, the success of marriages, and most of all, simply to praise God. To pray experimentally in these ways grows out of and affirms the vitality of our relationship with God and the reality of the dialogue of prayer.

About the divine reply in the dialogue of prayer the psalmists are certain. God answers when we call. God promises to his people, "I answer everyone who invokes me" (91:15), and the people respond that it is true. "[Yahweh] bends down to listen to me when I call" (116:2) and "hears me when I call to him" (4:3). Of course, in the Psalms the hearing and answering in which the singers rejoice is more than just listening or speaking. It is also action. Certainly we should expect to receive messages in response to our speaking, questioning, and listening, and we will have them. But very often when the Bible talks of God hearing or answering prayer, it means that the Listener has also become the Deliverer. God's answering means rescue, help, and healing. It means new strength, wisdom, and peace. The fact that God answers means, above all, that the Eternal One does indeed penetrate our little fractions of time with love and concern, so that our praying is a great deal more than just getting things off our chests. Because God answers when we call, we can pray with great expectancy.

Praying expectantly is essential to the life of prayer, but for many people it is also very difficult "What happens when it doesn't work?" they want to know, and it is a question that comes to anyone who prays. I share with them the puzzlement and sometimes the anguish of not seeing the things we have prayed about happen. Sometimes we can see that we have prayed selfishly or outside God's will and can grant that God's goodness has protected us from ourselves. But at other times apparently unanswered prayer seems to be a mystery, and we should accept that rather than fall into blaming. It is not necessarily a failure of technique or a failure of faith (though that is sometimes involved), and it is certainly not a failure of God's love or power. Apparent failures in prayer do not yield easily to simplistic or mechanical answers.

When prayer doesn't seem to "work," experiencing prayer as conversing with God can help us very much. It helps us to know that prayer is not a transaction, but a relationship. We are not bargaining, and we are quite mistaken to keep scorecards, judging the value of prayer and the faithfulness of God by a sort of batting percentage. What the lament songs have already taught us also helps us here. They accuse, "I call all day, my God, but you never answer" (22:2) and ask the anguished questions "Why?" and "How long, O Lord?" Yet all of this goes forward in a climate of confidence side by side with continuing declarations of trust. Those I know who know the most about prayer and who are effective intercessors freely admit their own experiences of apparent failure and their puzzlement over them. Yet they, too, refuse to abandon prayer or to give up. In prayer they ask God about their puzzlement, hoping to learn more of God's will and of the ways of prayer. They are patient, knowing that persistence in prayer is often more valuable than instant solutions. Yet above all, because they know God intimately, they continue, even in the face of mystery, to rest confidently in God's love and power. They know through experience, despite others' transactional scorecards, that God does indeed answer when we call.

To discover that prayer is an expectant dialogue creates extraordinary opportunities for our ordinary living. Learning to converse with God delivers us from just "saying prayers," from bargaining, and from magic, and brings us instead to a place where, simply and sincerely, we can share our whole lives with our Eternal Friend. As we steadily listen and answer, as we express our longing and our pain, our trust and our praise, we, too, can say with joyful confidence, "I call to you, O God, and you answer me."

SEVEN

CELEBRATING

Let earth praise Yahweh:
sea-monsters and all the deeps.
Let everything that breathes praise Yahweh.

Psalms 148:7; 150:6

One of the most unusual sermons ever recorded is the one Brother Anthony preached to a crowd of fish.[1] Actually Anthony had been trying to preach to the heretics at Rimini, but when they persisted in ignoring him, God gathered an attentive audience of fish, to rebuke them, just as in the Old Testament he had used a talking donkey to shame Balaam. *The Little Flowers of St. Francis* describes quite a sight. Schools of fish of all varieties and sizes crowded together and arranged themselves peacefully, the smallest in front to the largest at the outer edges. With "their heads a bit out of the water, gazing intently on St. Anthony's face, they waited eagerly to hear the word of God which the local heretics refused." When Anthony dismissed them with a blessing, the great throng of fish "all swam away to various parts of the sea, rejoicing and expressing their joy and applause in amazing games and gambols."

Here I like to imagine dolphins playfully stitching their way through the water and great blue whales bursting into the air, escorted by a platoon of giddy cod. I cannot help but connect this almost outrageous picture with Psalm 148 as it urges the sea monsters and all creation to praise God.

Undoubtedly, many readers are poised even now to attack all this as mere madness and to be done with it. To the modern, unimaginative ear there is, without question, a sort of craziness here. But it is a craziness that is far more prominent, far more instructive, and much less odd than we might at first think. From it we can learn a great deal about one of the most natural and inescapable movements of the heart before God—the life of thanksgiving and praise.

Rivers Clap Their Hands

One of the many ways in which the creation responds to God (*see also* chapter 3) is to sing and cry out for joy and to leap and clap its hands at the sight of its Maker coming in goodness and justice. This theme appears commonly enough in the Bible that we know it is more than a curiosity. Psalms 96 and 98, for example, invite the sea to thunder approval, the rivers to clap their hands, the fields to exult, and the forests and mountains to shout for joy at the announcement that Yahweh is coming to rule the world with justice. Similarly, Psalm 148 calls everything in creation to praise God, from the waters above the heavens to the seas under the earth and everything in between—sun, moon, and stars, mountains and hills, apples and cedars, snakes and eagles, all animals and weather, and people from every station of life. The song of Shadrach, Meshach, and Abednego in the fiery furnace gives an even more exhaustive catalog of the creatures who are called to "bless the Lord" and "give glory and eternal praise to him" (Daniel 3:51-90 [Apocrypha]).

One of the most striking New Testament occurrences of this theme is in the Book of Revelation. John describes in his vision the great festival of praise led by the elders and the myriad of angels surrounding the throne. In the midst of these choruses of adoration, he says, "Then I heard all the living things in creation—everything that lives in the air, and on the ground, and under the ground, and in the sea, crying, 'To the One who is sitting on the throne and to the Lamb, be all praise, honour, glory and power, for ever and ever'" (Revelation 5:13).

I am tantalized by the report that people who have had near-death experiences often tell of hearing music rising from the earth. However we may receive such reports, we may wonder whether in their brush with the Eternal they may have caught a glimpse of what John saw.

The most entertaining picture of the creation caught up in praise comes from Jesus himself. During his triumphant parade toward Jerusalem, the disciples crowding around Jesus infuriated the Pharisees by praising God joyfully "at the top of their voices." When the Pharisees urged Jesus to quiet them, he replied, "I tell you, if these keep silence the stones will cry out" (see Luke 19:35-40). Imagine how the Pharisees would have blanched had those rocky hillsides broken into strains of the ancient processional song, "Lift up your heads, O ye gates," with the olive trees adding counterpoint on "and the king of glory shall come in" (24:7)! It would have been impossible on this occasion for the creation not to praise God!

Of course, you may object, the stones did not cry out. Perhaps so. But maybe they did. Maybe they were singing wildly and laughing and shouting for joy, just as in the Psalms, because they saw the victory of God at hand. They had seen the Messiah, the Chosen One. The wind and waves knew to obey him, why not the hills and rocks and trees to praise him?

True, most of us don't quite hear the song or see the dance. At the same time I believe that there is something more than mere metaphor here, that it is perfectly reasonable to imagine that the creation can respond to its Maker. Almost without fail, when I have spoken publicly on this subject, several people have come to me afterward to exclaim, "I'm so glad to finally hear someone talk about this. I've been experiencing and feeling it for years, but have been afraid to say much about it." They usually go on to describe the rejoicing they have sensed in the trees, or from the plants in their gardens, or in the rivers and the sea. They have experienced what Isaac Watts once described in one of his hymns, "There's not a plant or flower below But makes your glories known."[2] I, too, have mused, often a bit timidly, that music seems to be built into creation. Beyond the strains easily heard, is it mere happenstance that melodies can spring from reeds and wood, from horsehair, gut, and metal? Or has the Creator planted deep in all of creation "the music of the spheres"? Regardless of how we may receive such reflections and the many scriptural references to creation's song, the vivid extravagance of the Bible at this point can give new depth and texture to our understanding of praise.

The Habit of Thanksgiving

One of the most beneficial experiments that I have undertaken in studying the Psalms has been to note specifically the many reasons why the psalmists praise or thank God. Seeing why all the creatures and the faithful celebrate God (145:10) has sharpened my ability to recognize grace in my own life. Often the singers thank God, for example, for having rescued them from a bad situation, as in the refrain in Psalm 107, "Then they called to Yahweh in their trouble and he rescued them from their sufferings. . . . Let these thank Yahweh for his love, for his marvels on behalf of men" (107:6, 8). The preceding Psalm describes how Israel sang praise for deliverance from Egypt, but also notes how quickly they forgot God and turned to grumbling (106:12-14, 21-25). Both their ready thanksgiving and their forgetful grumbling remind us that, thoughtless as it seems, it is easy to plead with God for help but fail to be thankful for it, or sometimes even to recognize it, when it comes. The Gospels, for example, recount how out of ten persons healed of leprosy, only one remembered to thank Jesus for healing him (Luke 17:11-19). We know that we should not judge them too harshly, for in relief, excitement, or anticipation of what still lies ahead, we, too, easily overlook thanksgiving. When we have prayed for wisdom or guidance, it is easy to congratulate ourselves on a successful outcome with *Well, I handled that all right.* Or when God has answered our prayers to protect us or meet our financial needs, we too often think, *That worked out pretty well,* or, *Wasn't that lucky?* We must always be on the lookout for our own ingratitude.

One way to guard against thanklessness is to keep a specific record of what requests we have brought to God and the answers we have received. Such a prayer journal is simple to keep and has the dual values both of prompting us to pray more specifically and of jogging our memories about God's goodness. It helps us to see God's response more clearly and to rise more eagerly to praise. Without being attentive in ways like this, we too easily misinterpret God's work on our behalf as merely happenstance, good fortune, or even worse, the fruit of our own wisdom and energy.

Another step toward gratitude is to consciously replace the habit of complaint with the habit of thankfulness. All of us, of course, have known persons who complain with such constant fervency that we wonder if they see grumbling as their God-given vocation. Some may adopt the life of complaint consciously, perhaps thinking perpetual discontent to be a mark of sophistication. But most of us, I suspect, fall into it carelessly. Certainly perfectionists, for whom nothing is ever completely right, are susceptible, tending to see the flaw or the one thing lacking rather than focusing on the beautiful and the good. Yet it seems to be part of our humanity, tracing back as far as Eden, to see the one thing forbidden rather than the abundance that has been given, to see shadows rather than light. When we allow this to be our habit, we deny God's goodness and hurt ourselves. I don't know anyone who is terminally grumpy and is also genuinely happy.

"It seems to be part of our humanity, tracing back as far as Eden, to see the one thing forbidden rather than the abundance that has been given, to see shadows rather than light. When we allow this to be our habit, we deny God's goodness and hurt ourselves."

We can defeat grumpiness by establishing a habit of gratitude. Most of us observe Thanksgiving Day (though even this prompts murmuring and whining in some), but we can go well beyond a nationally recognized celebration to creating little festivals of our own. They're not illegal, after all, and they can increase our ability to celebrate God's goodness, not only on special occasions, but also day by day. On our kitchen wall we have a colorful poster bearing the words, "We are thankful for . . . ," on which we and our children write specific reasons for thanksgiving. In the course of each day, it is helpful to take time to answer the question, "What do I thank God for today?" The psalmists, for example, thank God for generously providing for life itself. "He provides for all living creatures," they sing (136:25), drawing attention to what we so casually overlook, particularly in times of good health and economic security. The One who feeds all the creatures with a "generous hand" (145:15-16) is also the One who grants and sustains life in each moment. The habit of thanksgiving is particularly helpful because it reminds us of God's grace in what may seem routine. For example, giving thanks for each meal, far more than simply perpetuating a childhood ritual, can remind us daily of God's goodness. We can make such practices habits without letting them become merely routine. In our family, we thank God for our meals in a variety of ways. Sometimes we pray aloud, sometimes we sing, or sometimes we pause in silence. At other times I have found that looking at my meal while giving thanks for it makes my gratitude more vivid. I am consciously grateful not only for its nourishment, but also for its color, texture, variety, and fragrance, as well as for the people and places around the world that have had a hand in providing it. In our daily rounds we can easily praise the Lord for our friends, for the electricity that runs our machines, for the stranger who jump started the car, and for the little girl across the street who sings and laughs while she skates down the sidewalk. With practice we can even learn the habit of thanking God for work, for committee meetings, for a yard to mow, for garbage to take out, and for strength to wash the windows.

The habit of thankfulness is not simply another device for keeping a "positive mental attitude." Even though it does lift our spirits, the point is not to trick ourselves into cheerfulness, but to recognize the reality that God's "generous kindness" (145:7) is always near us. When we bog down in habits of petty complaint and routine gloominess, by our actions we deny the goodness of God. When we praise God's goodness, we are always right! How much better to rejoice in such love rather than grump our way through life, pretending that it is not so!

Loving God Back

Beneath the daily reasons for gratitude there lies a still deeper motive for praise and worship. A compelling urge to praise rises from the inescapable tug of God's love. "Yahweh's tenderness embraces all his creatures" (145:9), and as leaves turn toward sunlight, so the whole creation turns to its Source, knowing that it is endlessly loved by the Giver of Life. Indeed, this love is so great that one suspects that God's desire to create anything flows out of a surfeit of love, that creation exists so that its Maker will have something on which to lavish love.

If love is indeed a primary motive for praise, then not receiving and appreciating God's love may well be why praise is so often weak and tepid. Praise that is offered only out of duty can hardly be sturdy and joyful. It is true, of course, that the Bible does command us to praise God, but it is not because the Almighty thrives on compliments or needs an ego massage in order to be happy. The command to praise is given for our sake. Praise helps us to keep our perspective and to see things as they really are. Just mouthing the words of praise, even when we don't feel them rising naturally, can help us by calling attention again to God's love and care for us. Praise helps restore our spirit of celebration.

In a period of grade-A grumpiness a few years ago I experienced such a renewal of joy. In the early summer, bereft of the daily adulation of my students and consigned to pulling weeds in the flower garden, among other imagined or real troubles, I had for several days been in a mood of deep melancholy, scarcely able to enjoy life or praise God. Halfway through the flower garden, I remembered the constant refrain of Psalm 136, "His love is everlasting," and how it is repeated after each recollection of God's goodness as Creator and Deliverer. I decided to try it. Dutifully, at first, I began to thank God for the creation, for the garden, for the lovely trees, for my health, for my family, for salvation, for rescue in the dark valleys of graduate school, and so on, repeating aloud after each phrase, "His love is everlasting." To my surprise, what began as a dutiful experiment blossomed into a joyful occasion of worship. The words of praise were transformed into the spirit of celebration as I was taught anew the depth of God's love.

"Adoration is to be so taken by God's tenderness that we can never quite say 'I love you' well enough."

To see such boundless love can lead only to worship and adoration. In strains of praise we are eager to join the heavenly chorus singing, "You are our Lord and our God, you are worthy of glory and honour and power, because you made all the universe and it was only by your will that everything was made and exists" (Revelation 4:11). Basking in the sheer delight of being overwhelmed by love, our hearts nearly burst with adoration.

"Adoration," writes Douglas Steere, "is 'loving back.' For in the prayer of *adoration* we love God for Himself, for His very being, for his radiant joy. . . . In adoration we enjoy God. We ask nothing except to be near Him. We want nothing except that we would like to give Him all."[3] Adoration is to be so taken by God's tenderness that we can never quite say "I love you" well enough.

Georges Bernanos, in *The Diary of a Country Priest*, captures how the poor priest aches to love God back adequately. Wanting to give God everything, but frustrated that he doesn't know how to give, he mourns, "Yet I would have wished to be once, just once, magnificently generous to You."[4] He knew the meaning of Isaac Watts' great hymn text, "Love so amazing, so divine, Demands my soul, my life, my all."[5] In adoration, our greedy selves wilt before all that has already been given, and we desire only to give ourselves wholly to God.

Whirling and Dancing

Even as we struggle to praise God as grandly as we desire, the Psalms guide us by suggesting that praise should be constant, unrestrained, and full of celebration.

"I will bless Yahweh at all times, his praise shall be on my lips continually," announces one singer (34:1), while another urges, "Let the saints . . . sing for joy on their beds" (149:5, NIV). The New Testament captures the same spirit in its instruction to be "always and everywhere. . . giving thanks to God" (Ephesians 5:20). In the shower or in the car, as we cook or as we walk, we can learn simple ways of praising God constantly. Perhaps it will be humming little songs of praise when we mow or joining in the Scriptures' words of adoration while we jog. The inner whispers of worship can be offered up anywhere until, like incense of old, they lift the fragrance of our devotion continually to God.

If Israel's praise was constant, it also was a bit rowdy, at least to some modern tastes. If to the sea's thunderous roar, the rivers' applause, and the mountains' joyful shouts, you add worshipers singing and dancing to the music of trumpets, reeds, lyres, and a whole percussion section, you ought to have a celebration of worship that would outstrip the imagination of even the most spectacular-minded producers of religious extravaganzas. Here we see worship enthusiastic, lavish, and unrestrained.

King David himself may have set a precedent for such extravagance when he joyfully brought the Ark of the Covenant up to Jerusalem. He was so pleased, we are told, that he "danced whirling round before Yahweh with all his might, wearing a linen loincloth round him." Apparently this priestly garment could be dangerously revealing, for when he arrived home, his wife Michal scolded him sharply for his buffoonery in dancing and for showing too much of the royal anatomy to the public. David's reply captures the extravagance of praise. "I was dancing for Yahweh, not for them," he said, and just to be sure she understood his point, he promised with an oath, "I shall dance before Yahweh and demean myself even more" (2 Samuel 6:12-23). David knew who his audience was, and that's all that mattered to him. To praise God extravagantly was more important than any cautions of propriety or reputation. He had no hesitation in giving himself wholly to God.

Please understand that I am not urging you, decked in a royal loincloth, to slavishly imitate David during Sunday morning worship. But I am insisting that we should freely give ourselves to God in praise. Let there be unrestrained words and songs and festal shouts of religious words like *"Wow!"* Let there be hand clapping, foot stomping, dancing and leaping, laughter and unchecked grins. I am sure many readers shudder even now at such a prospect. But if we never, even in private, overcome the bonds of ego and inhibition in order to give ourselves in unbridled praise, of whatever form, we will never fully discover what it means to give ourselves wholly to God. Experiment with enthusiasm and extravagance in the life of worship. Examine carefully the inner constraints to see whether they resist the abandonment to God to which we are called.

Worship in private and in small groups can help to give us the freedom we need. When we are alone we can praise God in anyway which seems fitting, whether it is to sing, to sit in silence, to leap and dance, to raise our hands, or to fall prostrate on the floor. We generally don't experience such liberty in public worship, since most churches, whether prim and proper or loud and rowdy, tend to dictate both the content and style of worship. Private worship is one of the best places to get in tune with how we are encountering God personally and to experiment with how we can best offer ourselves completely in adoration. One of my students has often told me that this is one of the reasons he loves plowing the wheat fields back home. Alone on a tractor in the middle of a section of land, he can cheer (rather like the biblical word *exult*), pray, and worship in any other way that the Spirit prompts. Because of the liberty it affords, private worship is indispensable to the life of celebration.

Since celebration cannot be fully experienced alone, however, we need others to join us in liberated praise. Many small groups gather for this purpose, I am sure. We have come together in our home on Friday evenings for some time now, with only two ground rules. First, our sole purpose is to worship. (It is not a "Bible study.") Second, this worship is to go forward in complete freedom, one that many of us have seldom found in our own churches. Over the months, this little pocket of praise has welcomed individuals from a wide variety of congregations and denominations, for we have discovered together how much our lives are deepened when we can celebrate God without constraint.

The Sea Monsters' Chorus

If we were to content ourselves that words and songs, however extravagant, complete the life of praise, we would be badly mistaken. Though they are necessary and wonderful, they are not enough. Beyond all words, the impulse of our hearts, which compels us to thank and praise God, finally requires that our lives themselves be transformed into a great "Hallelujah!" The way we receive our lives and live them can become constant praise. When Saint Francis spoke of Brother Sun and Sister Moon, he was pointing to a fact of our lives which we easily overlook. In his amazing gentleness toward all creation, Francis was reminding us that we are kin to all the creatures, even though we have tended to distance ourselves from these, our relatives. We have mistakenly thought that because humankind has been granted stewardship over the natural order or because we have been fashioned in God's image that we have escaped our creatureliness. Genuinely impressive human achievements in science, technology, and the arts have heightened this illusion. But the fact remains that we, like the galaxies and the gnat, like Brother Sun or Cousin Coon, are creatures, as fully dependent on the hand of the Lord as they are.

We come closer to the truth by recognizing our creatureliness, but to delight in it transforms our lives, for rejoicing in the fact that we are God's creatures strikes directly at the heart of pride and sin. The human offense in the Garden of Eden was not, after all, a problem over sex and applesauce. It was the refusal to acknowledge our place in creation. "You shall be like God," the serpent coaxed, and in our naiveté we bought the line. And we still buy it. We would much rather be the Creator than the creature. In a time when we are encouraged to "not be beholden to anybody," to "look out for Number One," and to admire those who brag of doing it "my way," dependence has almost become a dirty word. Yet rejoicing that we, like all the rest of creation, depend on God doesn't shackle us. It frees us from the deceit and burden of trying to maintain a universe of our own.

One way of celebrating our own creatureliness is to join the sea monsters' chorus. Psalm 148's invitation to every sort of person to unite with the sea monsters and all creation in praising God is our invitation, too. It is more than a trick of imagination to discover that, by sharing the creation's songs, we come to rejoice more fully in our own creaturehood. I have shouted, "Amen!" to the sea's bass roar. I have whistled, "You are worthy, Lord!" with the warbler and the finch. I have clapped my hands with the waving limbs of the trees and with the rest of my created kin who are caught up in praise to God. As I have listened to and joined in their refrains, I have wanted to sing along with Francis, "Be praised, my Lord, in what you have created," so that finally, joyfully dependent, my life itself can be a hearty, peaceful "Yes!" to the One in whom "we live, and move, and have our being" (Acts 17:28, KJV).

We also shout a "Yes!" of praise by shaping our lives to fulfill God's purposes as completely as possible. Such an act is not, of course, merely a grudging submission to God's will. It is, instead, giving ourselves to God in great admiration and eagerness, because the divine purposes for us and for the world seem so unbelievably good. So as we fashion our lives as a cheer of "Yes!" to God, we reach out to fill our own place as creatures as completely as we can. We no longer need to dominate or take pride of place in respect to any other creature.

We can abandon the urge to rule at the office, at church, or at home. We can treat everything God has made with gentleness and generosity, rather than with grasping greed. In joyful dependence, we can grow to be as fully human as possible, as thoroughly in the image of God as we were intended to be. In reflecting the creativity and love of God, we can delight to sing and invent, to work and to love. We can write poetry and tell stories, show mercy to one another and make one another laugh. Having given up the burden of usurping the Creator's throne, we are now free to become who we are and to let our creaturely lives themselves, yielded gladly to God's will, shout praise to their Maker.

Even those who cannot somehow hear songs of praise in the rain dancing on the roof or in the evening breeze, even those have a place in creation's "Hallelujah Chorus." All those who delight, as creatures, to depend wholly on God and who eagerly shape their lives to do God's will have already added their voices to the song. Whether or not they can recognize it, all those who say "Yes!" to God with joy have already joined the sea monsters' chorus.

If, as in theology, devotion to God begins and ends in silence, then creation's choir, and we with it, may for a time fall into a holy hush. As the celebration crescendos to peaks of joy and wonder, we may open our mouths only to find that our hearts are shouting, but our lips are dumb. A sublime silence steals over each created thing, and in it comes a melting, a dissolving into love and reverence, into tears of joy and gratitude. It is not that creation won't sing again or that it refuses to sing now, but that it can't sing. In this moment the purest poetry and the sweetest melodies of praise simply cannot express God's overwhelming glory. Yet since we cannot bear to remain forever at such heights, the trees again will begin to clap, the seas to roar, and the sea monsters to sing out the refrain, all anticipating the day when, indeed, everything that breathes will praise the Lord.

STUDY GUIDE

Introduction

This study guide is not a fixed curriculum as such, but it does include resources that make it easily adaptable for both personal and group study. For each chapter of the book it includes supporting Bible readings, reflection questions, and ideas for songs that relate to the chapter's theme.

Bible Readings. The Bible readings for each chapter include seven psalms and seven other biblical portions. In general, the readings together support the theme of each of the chapters, though it is not unusual for a psalm to show a variety of themes. Readers could use these portions in a one-week reading program along with the book, or they could adapt them to a two-week or more schedule of readings. In the latter case, this could help support using the book as the basis of a quarter's study in a typical Sunday School schedule.

Questions for Study and Reflection. The reflection questions can be used profitably by individuals and groups. For personal study, a reader might want to write responses to or journal about the questions. Groups can use them to unfold their members' common insight and experience as they encounter the truth of the Bible. Perhaps these questions will stir up still others that will open your heart to hearing and addressing God through the Psalms.

Songs for Reading and Singing. The songs suggested are only a few of the many that are possible, since the songs known in the community of faith vary so widely. In keeping with the "all-time favorites" character of the Psalms themselves, we have chosen songs that are widely known and used in the Christian community. They are keyed to six prominent hymnals.* To these songs I hope you will add some of the less universally known but wonderful "new songs" that you use in your community of faith. Above all, I encourage you to sing, alone or together, for this is a fitting way to share the fact that we are learning again from Israel's songs.

*Key to Hymnals
Baptist—*The Baptist Hymnal*, 1991
Family of God—*Hymns for the Family of God*, 1976
Lutheran—*Lutheran Book of Worship*, 1978
Presbyterian—*The Presbyterian Hymnal*, 1990
Methodist—*The United Methodist Hymnal*, 1989
Worshiping Church—*The Worshiping Church*, 1990

ONE
LONGING

Bible Readings

Psalms 27, 42, 63, 84, 90, 119:169-176, 122

Mark 10:23-31; John 4:5-15; John 6:44-58; Ephesians 1:15-23; Ephesians 4:17-24; Philippians 3:7-14; Colossians 3:1-4, 16-17

Questions for Study and Reflection

1. Evelyn Underhill writes: "Mysticism is the passionate longing of the soul for God, the Unseen Reality, loved, sought and adored in Himself for Himself alone. . . . A mystic is not a person who practices unusual forms of prayer, but a person whose life is ruled by this thirst!" (p.105, "What Is Mysticism" in *Life As Prayer*) Think about people you know whose lives, by this definition, suggest that they are mystics. How much of a "mystic" do you think you are or could be?

2. In this chapter we have used several phrases or pictures to talk of eagerness for God: restlessness, thirst, wanting to see God's face. What other words or metaphors can you think of that would express that same eagerness or desire? Finish the sentence: "Delight in God is like. . . ."

3. Read and reflect on Psalm 73:25-26, which speaks of desiring God alone. What is the difference between devotion to God out of duty (perhaps in response to "You shall have no other gods

before me") and devotion to God out of desire? Which do you think is most like "Love the Lord your God with all your heart and with all your soul and with all your strength"?

4. ". . . this taste of knowing God stands as an invitation to enter and explore what now escapes even our imaginations" (p. 21). How would you describe or explain the continuing sense of adventure and discovery in our lives with God?

5. As aptly expressed in Abraham Heschel's book titled *God's Search for Man*, eventually we become aware that not only are we seeking God, but God is seeking us. Reflect on the ways that God in love has persistently pursued you, wooed you, called to you.

6. The chapter notes the sense of risk involved in encountering God "face to face" as expressed in the stories of Moses and Isaiah among others (pp. 34-35). Why do you think that our longing and eagerness for God might carry with it a sense of danger? How would you describe it?

7. What does recklessness or fanaticism feel like to you? How much do you think a fear of fanaticism, of going overboard, hinders people from abandoning themselves wholly to God? In what ways may that have hindered your own pursuit of God?

Songs for Reading and Singing
Jesus, Thou Joy of Loving Hearts
Family of God 451, Lutheran 356, Presbyterian 510, Worshiping Church 121

Jesus, the Very Thought of Thee
Baptist 225, Family of God 465, Lutheran 316, Presbyterian 310, Methodist 175, Worshiping Church 112

Be Thou My Vision
Baptist 60, Family of God 468, Presbyterian 339, Methodist 451, Worshiping Church 532

Spirit of God, Descend upon My Heart
Baptist 245, Family of God 147, Lutheran 486, Presbyterian 326, Methodist 500, Worshiping Church 290

TWO

WAITING

Bible Readings
Psalms 4, 37, 40, 46, 62, 130, 131

Isaiah 30:8-18; Isaiah 40:25-31; Lamentations 3:22-26;
Romans 8:18-27; Ephesians 3:14-21; Philippians 2:12-16;
James 5:7-11

Questions for Study and Reflection

1. In his book *Nurturing Silence in a Noisy Heart,* Wayne Oates writes of the many different kinds of "noises" that can distract us: the load of sound of external noises, the annoyance levels of particular sounds, "between-folks noises" caused by friction in relationships, "strange noises" in our hearts from past experiences, and more. What "noises," inward and outward, most hinder you from being attentive to God in your life or undermine a life of eager patience?

2. The concept of "sabbath" addresses both our need for patience and our need to yield control (pp. 56-57). How do you think the practice of sabbath could be helpful to you? What are some practical steps you could take to incorporate it in your life?

3. Gerald May writes in *Addiction and Grace* of the importance of spaciousness as an opening to God's work in our lives. What could you do to create a sense of spaciousness in your heart and life?

4. In a letter of spiritual counsel, Isaac Penington, a seventeenth-century Quaker leader, advised: "Do not look for such great matters to begin with; but be content to be a child, and let the Father proportion out daily to thee what light, what power, what exercises, what straits, what fears, what troubles he sees fit for thee; and do thou bow before him continually in humility of heart. Thou must join in with the beginnings of life, and be exercised with the day of small things, before thou meet with the great things, wherein is the clearness and satisfaction of the soul." How might we relate the concept of waiting with "the day of small things"?

5. Bernard of Clairvaux said, "Waiting upon God is not idleness, but work which beats all other work to one unskilled in it." Drawing on the chapter and on your experience, describe how waiting is action rather than inaction. Why do you think Bernard would call it "work"?

6. Why is it important to know that the interior life is "not a place that is taken by storm or violence"? (p. 44) What kinds of mistakes can knowing this guard us from?

7. What are some of the ways that you could "waste time for God"? How would you relate this idea to the classic statement that part of a person's purpose is "to enjoy God forever"? Do you think we should have to show some practical benefits to "wasting time for God"? Why or why not?

Songs for Reading and Singing
Have Thine Own Way, Lord
Baptist 294, Family of God 400, Methodist 382, Worshiping Church 584

Dear Lord and Father of Mankind
Baptist 267, Family of God 422, Lutheran 506, Presbyterian 345, Methodist 358, Worshiping Church 591

Near to the Heart of God
Baptist 295, Family of God 35, Presbyterian 527, Methodist 472, Worshiping Church 542

THREE
TREMBLING

Bible Readings
Psalms 8, 19, 29, 51, 99, 104, 139

Isaiah 6:1-8; John 1:14-18; 2 Corinthians 3:12-18;
2 Corinthians 12:1-4; Hebrews 12:18-29; Revelation
1:9-20; Revelation 22:1-9

Questions for Study and Reflection

1. Over the nearly 2,000 years of church history, many Christians have reported being so overwhelmed by the presence of God that it has evoked physical responses such as trembling, quaking, and stunned silences. Think about your own experiences of encounter, of the "fear of God," of "trembling." In what contexts did they happen? What prompted them? How did they affect you?

2. Why do you think people so often block or are shielded from experiences of genuine awe?

3. Noting the section "How Can It Be?" (p. 70), reflect on how we can hold together humankind's apparent insignificance with the Bible's teaching about their incomparable worth.

4. Paul briefly alludes to an experience in which he "heard things which must not and cannot be put into human language"

(pp. 63-64). What do you suppose those things could be? What do Paul's words suggest to you about the possibilities of spiritual experience?

5. For you, what things tend to make you stand in amazement before the love and power of God, tend to stir up in you a sense of awe? Of what value might it be to you to intentionally expose yourself to those things?

6. This chapter suggests that some people might tremble more in encountering God's love than in encountering God's power (p. 68), some because it is such overwhelmingly good news and some because they fear (or can't believe) being loved that much. Why do you think that might be so?

7. This chapter describes three responses in the Psalms to the ideal of a pure heart (pp. 75-76). When do each of these responses seem appropriate in your experience?

Songs for Reading and Singing
And Can It Be?
Baptist 147, Family of God 260, Methodist 363, Worshiping Church 473

Holy, Holy, Holy, Lord God Almighty
Baptist 2, Family of God 323, Lutheran 165, Presbyterian 138, Methodist 64, Worshiping Church 2

Spirit of the Living God
Baptist 244, Family of God 155, Presbyterian 322, Methodist 393, Worshiping Church 297

FOUR

DESPAIRING

Bible Readings
Psalms 6, 13, 22, 38, 44, 88, 137

Matthew 5:38-48; Luke 18:1-8; Luke 22:39-46; Acts 4:23-31;
Romans 8:35-39; 2 Corinthians 1:3-11; Hebrews 4:12-16

Questions for Study and Reflection

1. Matthew 27 tells us that Jesus, too, cried out to God with the words of Psalm 22, "My God, my God, why have you forsaken me?" In what ways can Jesus' cry at that point be encouraging or helpful to us in our times of despair?

2. Often Christians are encouraged to deny or suppress feelings of pain, puzzlement, and abandonment. Why do you think this is so?

3. Why is it important to ask the question "why?" in our times of crisis or puzzlement? Why is it okay not to have a tidy answer?

4. What are some of the ways that you have seen "death" invade life to weaken it and hollow it out? Why is it important to take this seriously as we try to relate the "inner life" to all of life?

5. This chapter suggests that "complaint," asking questions like "How long?" can actually be expressions of hope, ways of say-

ing that we haven't given in to thinking that God has abandoned us. It maintains communication rather than shuts it off. In what ways might you apply this insight helpfully in your own times of discouragement?

6. In the lament songs, what keeps honesty with God from degenerating into mere whining? (pp. 94-95) How does that teach us?

7. Once you understand the extravagance of the language about "enemies" in the Psalms, how much do you think these descriptions could be used of people who have become enemies to you? What do you find you most want to do—get even, ask God to get even for you, or ask God to forgive them?

Songs for Reading and Singing
Precious Lord, Take My Hand
Baptist 456, Family of God, 611, Presbyterian 404, Methodist 474, Worshiping Church 638

Out of the Depths
Lutheran 295, Presbyterian 240, Methodist 515, Worshiping Church 465

Come, Ye Disconsolate
Baptist 67, Methodist 510, Worshiping Church 613

I Want Jesus to Walk with Me
Baptist 465, Presbyterian 363, Methodist 521, Worshiping Church 642

STUDY GUIDE

FIVE

RESTING

Bible Readings
Psalms 23, 33, 91, 103, 107, 121, 136

Matthew 6:25-34; Philippians 4:4-9; Colossians 1:9-14;
1 Timothy 6:17-19; 2 Timothy 1:6-12; 1 Peter 5:5-11; 1 John 4:7-18

Questions for Study and Reflection

1. In what ways can you imagine God at work in "the real world"?
   Does a person of faith hold a different view of "the real world"
   than other people?

2. In what ways do we show that we often tend to trust ourselves
   and our own resources before we fall back on trusting God?
   How can we overcome that tendency?

3. This chapter urges recovering a sense of the wonder of God's
   creative and sustaining power (p. 106). Why is that important
   to nurturing trust?

4. What are some of the ways we might train ourselves to see God
   at work in our everyday lives?

5. Hannah Whitall Smith says that worry and trust are as incompatible as oil and water (p. 115). What truth does she identify
   in saying this? Would you qualify her statement in any way?
   Why or why not?

6. Using the psalms listed for this chapter and/or other psalms of trust, list the words or word pictures they use to portray trust. Which ones are especially meaningful for you?

7. What other words or word pictures (biblical or not) could be strong, helpful ones for you to describe what it means to trust or rest in God?

8. "Resting" or trust can have a double sense about it. On the one hand it can represent a shelter to protect us from what comes against us. On the other, it can represent a place of safety from which we can venture, from which we might dare to step into the new. At this point, which of these senses seems most helpful to you?

Songs for Reading and Singing
A Mighty Fortress
Baptist 8, Family of God 118, Lutheran 228, Presbyterian 259, Methodist 110, Worshiping Church 43

There's a Wideness in God's Mercy
Baptist 25, Family of God 115, Lutheran 290, Presbyterian 298, Methodist 121, Worshiping Church 486

O God, Our Help in Ages Past
Baptist 74, Family of God 370, Lutheran 320, Methodist 117, Worshiping Church 78

The Lord's My Shepherd
Family of God 40, Lutheran 451, Presbyterian 170, Methodist 136, Worshiping Church 330

SIX

CONVEYING

Bible Readings
Psalms 25, 61, 86, 116, 119:145-152, 142, 145

Exodus 33:7-17; Luke 11:1-12; John 15.1-7; Ephesians
6:10-20; Colossians 4:2-4; 1 Timothy 2:1-8; James 5:13-18

Questions for Study and Reflection
1. In your experience, how common is the sentiment that "prayer
    doesn't really accomplish anything?" (p. 120) Why do people
    (including people in the community of faith) hold such an
    opinion?

2. Through the centuries, many religious leaders have advised that
    people pray the Psalms. Because they are both songs and
    prayers, they can teach us and help us to pray. In what ways
    have the Psalms helped you to pray? In what ways do you antic-
    ipate that they will be helpful? What hindrances do you find in
    "praying the Psalms"?

3. The Bible and many experienced teachers describe prayer as a
    dialogue, a two-way conversation. In what ways do your under-
    standing and experience need to grow in order to enjoy this
    more fully? Describe the ways in which you already have found
    the dialogue of prayer rewarding.

4. Why would it be helpful to "wait," as William Penn suggests (pp. 125-126), when we come to God in prayer? How in practical terms can we act on Penn's counsel?

5. The Psalms represent a more liturgical or formal type of prayer, but the Bible has other types as well. For example, look at the models of "prose prayer" in the Bible: the prayers of Abraham (Genesis 18:22-33), Moses (Exodus 33:12-23, Numbers 14:10-25, and others), Elijah (1 Kings 19:9-18), and others in the Old Testament or the prayers of Jesus in the New Testament. How do they illustrate the dialogue of prayer?

6. In what ways is prayer really a response? Do we initiate prayer, or does God?

7. To pray "Thy will be done" is an invitation to transformation much more than it is trying to get God to agree to a transaction, to do our will. Do you think knowing this may make us cautious about prayer? How much do you think we resist prayer because we know that, as Richard Foster says, "to pray is to change"?

Songs for Reading and Singing
What a Friend
Baptist 182, Family of God 466, Lutheran 439, Presbyterian 403, Methodist 526, Worshiping Church 622

Lord, Speak to Me, That I May Speak
Baptist 568, Family of God 625, Lutheran 403, Presbyterian 426, Methodist 463, Worshiping Church 574

Sweet Hour of Prayer
Baptist 445, Family of God 439, Methodist 496, Worshiping Church 623

SEVEN

CELEBRATING

Bible Readings
Psalms 65, 93, 96, 100, 146, 148, 150

2 Samuel 6:12-22; Luke 19:28-40; Ephesians 5:1-20;
1 Peter 2:9-10; Revelation 4:1-11; Revelation 5:6-14;
Revelation 7:9-17

Questions for Study and Reflection

1. In what ways have you sensed (or could you imagine) all of creation praising God? How can that enhance our praise?

2. What times or occasions in your life might become times of habitual (without being legalistic) thanksgiving? Include daily opportunities as well as seasonal or special occasions.

3. Do you find that people around you think it is sophisticated or socially desirable to be critical? What other roots would you identify for frequent criticism? How does this undercut celebration?

4. The psalms of praise that are classified as "hymns" typically answer at least three questions: who is called to praise, how praise is to be offered, and why God is to be praised (frequently introduced by the words "for," "since," or "who"). Using Psalms 145–150, all "Hallel Psalms," songs of praise characterized by the use of "Hallelujah," list the various ways in which these three questions are answered.

5. Douglas Steere describes adoration as "loving God back" (p. 148). How can or does that become part of the rhythm of your response to God?

6. In what ways can you imagine nurturing the dance, singing with the sea monsters, and giving rein to extravagance in your personal life with God? In corporate life and worship?

7. Reflect on how your life itself can be a shout of praise, a hallelujah, to God. What might you do to make sure that it is so?

Songs for Reading and Singing

All People That on Earth Do Dwell
Baptist 5, Family of God 381, Lutheran 245, Presbyterian 220, Methodist 75, Worshiping Church 317

All Creatures of Our God and King
Baptist 27, Family of God 347, Lutheran 527, Presbyterian 455, Methodist 62, Worshiping Church 356

Praise to the Lord, the Almighty
Baptist 14, Family of God 337, Lutheran 543, Presbyterian 482, Methodist 139, Worshiping Church 77

NOTES

Introduction

1. D. Elton Trueblood, *The Trustworthiness of Religious Experience* (Richmond, Ind.: Friends United Press, 1979), 48-49.

Chapter 1

1. Augustine, *The Confessions of St. Augustine,* trans. John K. Ryan (Garden City, N.Y.: Doubleday and Co., 1960), 255.
2. As quoted in Evelyn Underhill, *The Mystics of the Church* (New York: George H. Doran Co., n.d.), 151.
3. Anonymous, *The Little Flowers of St. Francis,* ed. and trans. Raphael Brown (Garden City, N.Y.: Doubleday and Co.,1971), 43.
4. Sören Kierkegaard, *Purity of Heart,* trans. Douglas V. Steere (New York: Harper and Row, 1938).
5. *Juan* Carlos Ortiz, *Disciple* (Carol Stream, Ill.: Creation House, 1975), 81.
6. Underhill, *Mystics of the Church,* 12-13.
7. Frederick Buechner, *The Sacred Journey* (San Francisco: Harper and Row, Publishers, 1982), 77-78.
8. Frank C. Laubach, *Letters by a Modern Mystic* (New York:Student Volunteer Movement, 1937), 12, 32, 41.
9. *The Way of a Pilgrim,* trans. R.M. French (New York: Ballantine Books, 1974).
10. As quoted in William L. Vaswig, *At Your Word, Lord* (Minneapolis: Augsburg Publishing House, 1982) 20; *see also* Agnes Sanford, *Sealed Orders* (Plainfield, N.J.: Bridge Publishers, 1972), 107.
11. Anonymous, *Little Flowers,* 247-248.
12. C.S. Lewis, *The Weight of Glory,* ed. Walter Hooper, rev. ed. (New York: Macmillan Publishing Co., 1980), 34.

Chapter 2

1. Quoted in Richard J. Foster, *Celebration of Discipline* (San Francisco: Harper and Row, 1978), 16.
2. Quoted in Henri J.M. Nouwen, *Out of Solitude* (Notre Dame, Ind.: Ave Maria Press, 1974), 55.
3. Jeanne Guyon, *Experiencing the Depths of Jesus Christ,* 3rd ed. (Goleta, Calif.: Christian Books, 1975), 63.
4. Kenneth Leech, *True Prayer* (San Francisco: Harper and Row, 1981), 10.
5. Evelyn Underhill, *Light of Christ* (Wilton, Conn.: Morehouse-Barlow Co., 1981), 33.
6. Henri J.M. Nouwen, *Clowning in Rome* (Garden City, N.Y.: Doubleday and Co., 1979), 53.
7. George Fox, *The Journal of George Fox,* ed. John L. Nickalls (Cambridge: Cambridge University Press, 1952), 346.
8. Nouwen, *Clowning in Rome,* 88.
9. Douglas V. Steere, *Prayer and Worship* (New York: Association Press, 1938), 23-24.
10. Shelly, Maynard, "Try *Gelassenheit,*" *The Mennonite,* 97:22 (October 26, 1982), 509-510. Quoted by Martin Marty in *Context,* 14 January 15, 1983), 2:2.

11. Henri J.M. Nouwen, *The Genesee Diary* (Garden City, N.Y. Doubleday and Co., 1981), 148.
12. D. Meister Eckhart, *Meister Eckhart,* trans. Raymond B. Blakney (New York: Harper and Row, 1941), 16.
13. Evelyn Underhill, *Abba* (Wilton, Conn.: Morehouse-Barlow Co., 1982), 32-33.
14. Quoted in *An Anthology of Devotional Literature,* ed. Thomas S. Kepler (Grand Rapids: Baker Book House, 1977), 335.
15. Abraham Joshua Heschel, *The Sabbath* (New York: Farrar, Straus, and Giroux, 1975), 3.
16. Jean-Pierre de Caussade, *The Sacrament of the Present Moment,* trans. Kitty Muggeridge (San Francisco: Harper and Row, 1982), 22.

Chapter 3
1. Elizabeth Barrett Browning, *Aurora Leigh* (New York: Thomas Y. Crowell Co., 1900), 268.
2. Reginald Heber, "Holy, Holy, Holy," *Great Hymns of the Faith,* ed. John W. Peterson (Grand Rapids, Mich.: Singspiration Music, 1968), 70.
3. Robert Grant, "O Worship the King," ibid., 1.
4. Isaac Watts, "Joy to the World," ibid., 87.
5. Thomas Merton, *On the Psalms* (London: Sheldon Press, 1977), 6.
6. Sören Kierkegaard, *The Prayers of Kierkegaard,* ed. Perry D. LeFevre (Chicago: University of Chicago Press, 1956), 5.
7. William Temple, *Daily Readings from William Temple,* comp. Hugh C. Warner, ed. William Wand (New York: Abingdon Press, 1965), 56.
8. Benedicta Ward, ed., *The Desert Christian* (New York: Macmillan Publishing Co., 1975), 55.

Chapter 4
1. C.S. Lewis, *Reflections on the Psalms* (New York: Harcourt, Brace and World, 1964), 22-25.
2. Maltbie D. Babcock, "This Is My Father's World," *Great Hymns of the Faith,* ed. John W. Peterson (Grand Rapids, Mich.: Singspiration Music, 1968), 39.
3. Claus Westermann, *Praise and Lament in the Psalms,* trans. Keith R. Crim and Richard N. Soulen, rev. ed. (Atlanta: John Knox Press, 1981), 260-65.

Chapter 5
1. J. Hudson Taylor, "The Call to Service," *Perspectives on the World Christian Movement,* ed. Ralph D. Winter and Steven C. Hawthorne (Pasadena, Calif.: William Carey Library, 1981), 238.
2. John Greenleaf Whittier, "Dear Lord and Father of Mankind," *Great Hymns of the Faith,* ed. John W. Peterson (Grand Rapids, Mich.: Singspiration Music, 1968), 358.
3. Hannah Whitall Smith, *The Christian's Secret of a Happy Life* (Old Tappan, N.J.: Fleming H. Revell Co., 1942), 54.
4. Thomas Kelly, *The Eternal Promise* (New York: Harper and Row, 1966), 58.
5. David and Karen Mains, *The God Hunt* (Elgin, Ill.: David C. Cook, 1984).
6. Smith, *Christian's Secret,* 53.
7. Ibid., 52-53.

Chapter 6
1. Frank Laubach, *Prayer: The Mightiest Force in the World* (New York: Fleming H. Revell Co., 1946), 76.
2. Moshe Greenberg, *Biblical Prose Prayer* (Berkeley: University of California Press, 1983), 36-37.
3. Anonymous, *The Little Flowers of St. Francis,* ed. and trans. Raphael Brown (Garden City, N.Y.: Image Books, 1958), 256-57, 278.

4. Jean-Nicholas Grou, *How to Pray,* trans. Joseph Dalby (London: James Clarke and Co., 1955), 19.
5. Caroline Emelia Stephen, *Quaker Strongholds,* 3rd ed. (London: Edward Hicks, 1891), 83.
6. Douglas V. Steere, *Prayer and Worship* (New York: Association Press, 1938), 19.
7. William Penn, *No Cross, No Crown,* ed. Ronald Selleck (Richmond, Ind.: Friends United Press, 1981), 45.
8. Thomas Kelly, *The Eternal Promise* (New York: Harper and Row, 1966), 77-78.
9. Steere, *Prayer and Worship,* 10.
10. Kenneth Leech, *True Prayer* (San Francisco: Harper and Row, 1980), 36.
11. *The Book of Common Prayer,* 1928 ed. (New York: Oxford University Press, 1952), 77.
12. Penn, *No Cross,* 40.
13. Greenberg, *Prose Prayer,* 17.
14. Thomas Kelly, *Reality of the Spiritual World* (Wallingford, Conn.: Pendle Hill, 1942), 36.
15. Henri J.M. Nouwen, *Clowning in Rome* (Garden City, N.Y.: Doubleday and Co., 1979), 7-71.
16. Laubach, *Prayer,* 67.
17. Ibid., 64.
18. Agnes Sanford, *The Healing Light* (St. Paul, Minn.: Macalester Park, 1947), and *The Healing Gifts of the Spirit* (Philadelphia: J.B. Lippincott Co., 1966), among others.

Chapter 7
1. Anonymous, *The Little Flowers of St. Francis,* ed. and trans. Raphael Brown (Garden City, N.Y.: Image Books, 1958), 131-33.
2. Isaac Watts, "We Sing the Mighty Power of God," *The Worshipbook* (Philadelphia: Westminster Press, 1972), 628.
3. Douglas V. Steere, *Prayer and Worship* (New York: Association Press, 1938), 34-35.
4. Georges Bernanos, *The Diary of a Country Priest,* trans. Pamela Morris (New York: Macmillan Co., 1937), 240.
5. Isaac Watts, "When I Survey the Wondrous Cross," *Worshipbook,* 635.

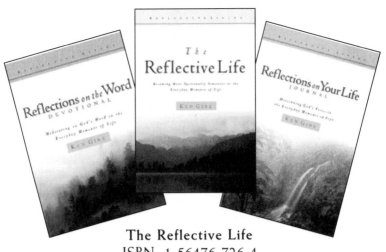

The Reflective Life
ISBN: 1-56476-726-4
$19.99 (U.S.)
Reflections on the Word
ISBN: 1-56476-751-5
$14.99 (U.S)
Reflections on Your Life
ISBN: 1-56476-725-6
$12.99 (U.S.)

The Reflective Life is the cornerstone of the "Reflective Living Series." It introduces readers to three habits that nurture a reflective life–reading, reflection, and response– and helps them apply these habits to their lives.

Reflections on the Word (Devotional) is designed to help readers develop the habit of slowing down to digest God's Word. This book features selected Scripture passages–as well as reflections and prayers not only from the author but from believers around the world and across the centuries.

Reflections on Your Life (Journal) helps readers apply the lifestyle described in *The Reflective Life* by recording what God is teaching them. Space is provided to record observations, prayers, and personal applications.

Ken Gire, the author of the "Reflective Living Series," is a graduate of Texas Christian University and Dallas Theological Seminary and formerly served as Director of Educational Products at Insight for Living. Ken and his family live in Colorado.